Backcountry Roads and Trails
San Diego County

Fourth Edition

Jerry Schad

Centra Publications
San Diego, California

Published by:
Centra Publications
P.O. Box 191029
San Diego, CA 92159

Trips described in this book:

1. PALOMAR MOUNTAINS
2. JULIAN
3. CUYAMACA MOUNTAINS
4. LAGUNA MOUNTAINS
5. ANZA-BORREGO DESERT

Area Map

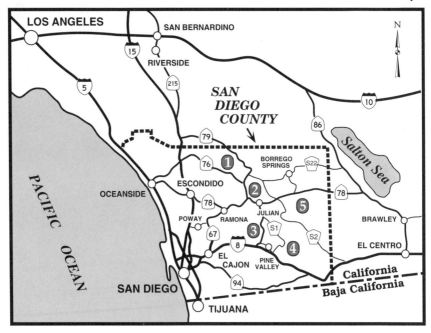

Contents

Stonewall Peak Trail

The Desert Experience   62

Trip 5: The Anza-Borrego Desert   65

Cholla cactus

Smoke tree in Fish Creek wash

DISCOVERING
SAN DIEGO COUNTY

In the minds of most outsiders, San Diego is a laid-back beach town with a pleasant Mediterranean climate. But this view is about as one-dimensional as the narrow strip of coastline it's usually applied to. Behind that narrow strip is the sprawling, businesslike patchwork quilt of houses and places of work that metropolitan San Diego has become. Out beyond even that spreads the three quarters of San Diego County that few visitors see, but many coastal residents consider as their back yard. This is San Diego's "backcountry," a sparsely populated and in places primeval region of chaparralled and forested mountains, and vast, empty desert spaces.

The county's borders are just broad enough in the east-west direction to encompass a truly amazing diversity of climate, terrain and vegetation. Inland about 30-50 miles from the coast stand the pine-crested mountain complexes known as the Palomar, Cuyamaca, and Laguna mountains—all accessible by paved road from the cities below. These and other mountains forming the county's backbone are a part of the Peninsular Ranges, which run the length of Baja California and stretch north into California as far as Orange and western Riverside counties. A bit farther east, some 60 miles or more from the coast, lies the low, hot, dry and colorful Anza-Borrego Desert, which itself slopes down to the sub-sea-level basin of the Salton Sea.

Perhaps no other county in the United States can offer so wide a range of recreational activity—year round. Traditionally winter through spring is *the* season for desert buffs, while the mountains are popular mostly in the late spring and summer. But don't let the "off-seasons" deter you. You can experience the bitter, wind-whipped chill of a snow-dusted mountain in midwinter, or the fury of the sun and desiccating heat of a midsummer's day in the desert. At these times especially, you'll find the peace and solitude you simply can't get down in the city.

Merely driving out to the backcountry is exciting, but not totally fulfilling. To really appreciate our local mountains and desert, you must temporarily abandon your vehicle and strike off on foot into a pine forest or a desert wash. Only in this way can you soak up their true essence. That's exactly what this book is about—a brief introduction to some of the finest of San Diego's backcountry trails, along with some driving tips to help you reach them.

There are five distinct "trips" in this book: Trips 1-4 are mountain areas within one or two hours driving time from San Diego. Trip 5, the Anza-Borrego Desert, requires about two hours' drive one-way. For each trip you will find a listing of campgrounds, picnic spots, points of interest, and appropriate phone numbers, as well as information on the paved highways leading into the area. Each trip section also features maps and descriptions of selected trails.

Desert sunflowers in Borrego Valley

The majority of the walks in this book are short and easy enough for the whole family to enjoy. A few are better for extended day hikes or even overnight backpacking. Adverse weather conditions (heavy snow in winter or heat in summer) might deter you from trying some of the longer trails, but on average San Diego County's weather is quite benign. Mountain-climbing skills aren't required for any of the hikes, but a moderate amount of physical conditioning is desirable.

The longer hikes described in this book keep well away from human habitation, so good preparation is important for those. Preparedness can make the difference between a pleasant experience on the trail and one which could prove to be, at best, miserable. These few suggestions may help:

Clothing and footwear. This includes warm clothing on cold days in the mountains. Temperatures may drop to below freezing, and strong winds are common in exposed areas. Remember to keep your extremities warm with a cap and mittens. On warm spring or summer days, don't go near-naked when out in the sun for a long time, even though you may feel most comfortable that way. That is the time of year when the sun's radiation reaches its peak intensity. Cover yourself up with loose fitting, light-colored clothes and a hat for protection from the sun's ultraviolet rays. When hiking in the desert, long pants will help keep the cactus spines at bay. Running or walking shoes are fine for most of the trails in this book, but it's better to wear lightweight hiking boots if you are prone to ankle twists when walking on uneven or rocky ground.

Water and nourishment. Water is generally not available along the trails, so take along all you'll need. That can range from a pint of water for a two-hour hike in 50° weather, to as much as a quart per hour when the temperature hits the 90° range. Quick-energy snacks are useful to stave off fatigue on the longer hikes.

A good psychological attitude. If you have young kids, never mind—they already have it. As an adult, try to shrug off any negative attitudes you may have carried with you from the city, and try to be open to unaccustomed sensory experiences. The rewards are many if you're open-eyed, open-eared, and open minded.

Further tips. Remember, when out on the trail, that you take on the burden of responsible use. Observe the backpacker's motto: "Take only memories, leave only footprints." Not everyone lives up to this ideal, and you may add to the enjoyment of those who follow by helping to remove and pack out any trash that has been thoughtlessly discarded by others.

Most of San Diego's backcountry is under the jurisdiction of the Cleveland National Forest or various state parks. This means that there are general prohibitions on collecting or removing animals, plants and minerals, and there may be restrictions on taking pets along certain trails.

The mountains of Southern California are especially vulnerable to destructive wildfires. For this reason, campfires are not allowed outside of the developed campgrounds. Also for this reason and others, never smoke on the trail, and make sure you discard any smoking materials in proper places, such as the ash tray inside your car.

Visitors to the Anza-Borrego Desert must observe regulations that are designed to protect its fragile environment and natural beauty. Naturalists estimate that it takes centuries for nature to restore some desert areas to their original condition once they've been denuded of vegetation. Off-road vehicles are one of the biggest culprits in that regard. In Anza-Borrego and elsewhere (except in areas specifically designated as off-road recreation sites) vehicles must be driven only on approved routes of travel. Desert campfires are not allowed unless built in containers, and the native vegetation, whether dead or alive, must never be used for fuel.

Aside from taking a few simple precautions and observing the special regulations, a day spent hiking in the mountains or deserts of San Diego County is little more trouble than a day's visit to the beach or Balboa Park. But a walk in the backcountry wilderness adds up to much more than just a diversion, an escape from the frantic cycles of modern living. It is a chance to get back in touch with your relationship to the world of rocks, trees, plants, clean air, and clear water. It is a moment of freedom, and a time of renewal.

This, then, is an invitation to the wonders that lie only a short distance away. Come explore this land, and learn to appreciate its many moods.

THE MOUNTAIN EXPERIENCE

For many San Diegans a trip to the mountains amounts to a drive up to Palomar for a look at its giant telescope, or to Julian for apple pie or cider. There's nothing wrong with this approach, but you're missing something if you don't have a chance to walk in the woods and along the streams, and to get some healthy exercise in the process. Walking in the mountains lets you escape from traffic, telephones, too many people in too little space, jarring noise of all sorts, and other pressures of city life. By walking with a clear mind, you can often gain a heightened awareness of your surroundings. Simple perceptions like the crunch of autumn leaves underfoot, the trill of bird, the song of wind in the swaying pine needles, or the sparkle of hoarfrost clinging to a branch in the early-morning sun can make your day, if not your whole week.

San Diego County has no ice-mantled peaks, no high-volume river, nor any famous trail to match the likes of the John Muir Trail atop the High Sierra. What it does have is surprisingly lush forests in spite of its generally arid climate, and startling changes of elevation and vegetation. Parts of Palomar and Cuyamaca have the same kinds of trees and other vegetation that grow on the mid-elevation slopes of the Sierra Nevada, even though our mountains lie hundreds of miles to the south. There's far less moisture to be sure, but nearly every ravine and canyon resounds with the sound of flowing water during the month or two following the heaviest winter storms. On the Laguna Mountain crest, you can stand in a pine forest that gets maybe 30-40 inches of rain a year and look down on hundreds of square miles of brown desert lucky to get one-tenth that much.

At the very least, our mountains offer a genuine opportunity to "get away from it all" with a minimum of travel commitment. Most of the trails included in this mountain section of the book are within only an hour's drive of metropolitan San Diego.

The four mountain areas I have chosen for this book combine the best of desirable features for the day hiker. All walks in this section are on public property—either a state or county park, or within the boundaries of the Cleveland National Forest.

Sugar pine cones

12

The mountains of San Diego County belong to the Peninsular Ranges, so named because they form the backbone of the Baja California peninsula. The extension of these ranges intrudes some 130 miles into the state of California, with the Santa Ana Mountains in Orange County and San Jacinto Mountains in Riverside County marking the northern limit. Major components in San Diego County include the forested Agua Tibia and Palomar Mountains, the Cuyamaca Mountains, and the Laguna Mountains, all of which are included in this section (Trips 1-4). The desert mountain ranges of the county, such as the Santa Rosa Mountains and Vallecito Mountains, are also part of the Peninsular Ranges; and hikes in these areas are treated in the desert section (Trip 5) of this book.

In the wetter, coastal portions of the Peninsular Ranges, the west-facing foothills are covered with dense chaparral. Oaks, sycamores, willows, and other riparian (or stream-loving) vegetation cluster along many of the canyon bottoms. At higher elevations of up to four or five thousand feet, oak trees and grasslands spread across the rolling terrain. Most territory above 5000 feet is well forested by oaks and various coniferous trees—pines, firs, and cedars. The east-facing slopes of the mountains tend to be steep and covered by either chaparral or high-desert vegetation.

A wide variety of wildlife exists today in the mountains as it always has, although not in the same great abundance. Residents of the middle and upper elevations include southern mule deer, raccoons, squirrels, gray foxes, striped and spotted skunks, and many kinds of birds. Predators, such as coyotes, bobcats, and even mountain lions, are relatively common, but almost always discreet in their behavior, and therefore seldom seen.

Human population in the mountains of San Diego County is thinly distributed, although a kind of low-density suburbanization in some areas is threatening their remote and peaceful character. Several thousand people reside in and around Julian, where a large portion of the acreage is privately owned. Julian has seen its heyday as a gold-boom town in the last century, and today it draws tourists by the thousands on weekends. Most of the mountainous territory in San Diego County 25 miles or more from the coast is maintained as open space for ranching purposes, or administered as park or public land by various state and federal agencies.

After a while, the allure of mountain pines and clear blue skies beckons even the most habitual city-dweller. So follow your inclinations and head for the mountains soon, and enjoy!

Trip 1
The Palomar Mountains

Facilities and Points of Interest:

Palomar Observatory (742-2119)

Cleveland National Forest (788-0250)
camp and picnic grounds:
  Fry Creek ▲ ⋔
  Observatory ▲ ⋔
  Oak Grove ▲
  Dripping Springs ▲ ⋔
  San Luis Rey ⋔

Palomar Mountain State Park (765-0755)
camp and picnic grounds:
  Doane Valley ▲
  Silver Crest ⋔

Palomar County Park (565-3600) ▲

La Jolla Indian Reservation (742-1297) ▲

The Palomar Mountain region holds a special fascination. Not only is this the most magnificently wooded area in all of San Diego County, but it also cradles atop its highlands one of the most important astronomical observatories in the world. The 200-inch Hale telescope at Palomar Observatory—once the world's largest—but soon to be only fourth or fifth largest—still remains an important tool for exploring the universe at large.

The Palomar Mountains (which I'm choosing to call them) are actually made up of several mountain ridges. The major ones are Palomar Mountain itself, on which the observatory is located; Aguanga Mountain, east of the observatory; and Agua Tibia Mountain, on the western end of the group. The point of highest elevation, east of Palomar Observatory, is unimaginatively dubbed High Point.

Parts of the Palomar Mountains were occupied by native American tribes long before the coming of European emigrants. Bedrock mortar holes in the granite of the mountain tell of the existence of inhabitants who relied heavily upon foods derived from ground-up acorns. These early dwellers called the area *Paauw*, a word meaning "pigeon roost." Band-tailed pigeons once nested in abundance on the slopes, and some can still be spotted today.

Thousands of acres of thickly-wooded uplands and gentle valleys in the Palomar Mountain region are within the jurisdiction of the Cleveland National Forest or the California Department of Parks and Recreation. Large portions are under private ownership, too, so you will want to observe any NO TRESPASSING signs while driving off the main roads or hiking around. Except for one trail that climbs Agua Tibia Mountain, all trails profiled here cover the prime woodlands atop Palomar Mountain itself.

The one and a half hour drive from San Diego to Palomar is always an interesting one, but especially nice when the air is clean and the visibility excellent. From Escondido, which is freeway-close to any urbanized part of San Diego, follow Valley Parkway and Valley Center Road (County Highway S-6) through the rolling,

Trip 1: Palomar Mountains

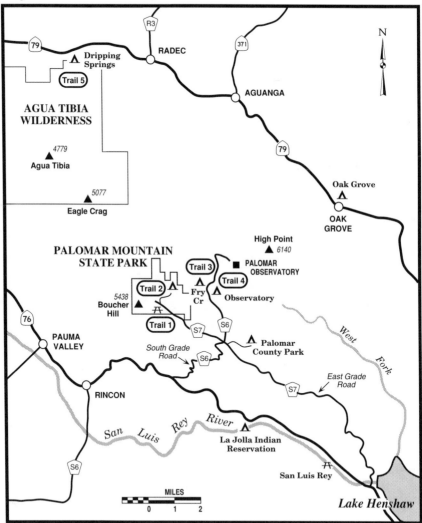

agricultural tableland of Valley Center and down to the valley of the San Luis Rey River at Rincon (State Highway 76). For a few miles the S-6 route joins with Highway 76; then it forks left as South Grade Road, which starts a relentless ascent of the mountain. You can either go that way, or else stay on 79 for a more circuitous approach via East Grade Road (County S-7). The former is steeper and more winding, while the latter offers a gentle, but longer, approach. I'd recommend going up one way and coming back down the other way to take maximum advantage of views in nearly every direction.

At the crossroads of S-6 and S-7 on top of the mountain, East Grade Road continues west along Palomar's main ridge to Palomar Mountain State Park, while S-6 runs past the National Forest campgrounds to the observatory. There's a store and cafe at the intersection.

From the North County coastal communities, you can take Highway 76, which follows the San Luis Rey River all the way from the coast to Lake Henshaw at the foot of the Palomar Mountains.

If you're a San Diego resident coming back down the mountain on East Grade Road, you may want to try swinging south on State Highways 76 and 79 toward Santa Ysabel, and then circle back to San Diego on Highway 78 by way of Ramona.

Palomar Observatory

On the Doane Valley Nature Trail

Trip 1, Trail 1
Scott's Cabin to Boucher Hill

Approximate distance: 3 miles for the loop
Elevation at trailhead: 5200 feet
Low point (Cedar Grove Campground):
  4840 feet
High point (Boucher Hill): 5420 feet

The Sierra Nevada-like atmosphere of Palomar Mountain State Park makes it a perfect retreat—even if only for a day. Overlooking a large part of Southern California from a mile-high altitude, the park consists of nearly 2000 acres of rolling timberland interspersed with gentle meadowland and deeply shaded ravines. A small network of paved roads and trails runs throughout the park, affording ample opportunity for leisurely exploration by car or on foot.

One possible trail loop begins near the park office at the entrance, and includes a visit to the ruins of Scott's Cabin and a view of the lowlands from Boucher Hill. Park in the large lot at Silver Crest Picnic Area, then pick up the trail across the road. Not much remains of the log cabin which was built by a little-known homesteader who once tended the old apple orchard near the park's entrance. From Scott's Cabin, the trail heads sharply downhill in thick woods to Cedar Grove Group Campground. You can continue on the Adams Trail, on the far side of the campground. I found it to be terrific right after a summer thunderstorm, which left bright orange Humboldt lilies wet and glistening by the trailside.

Adams Trail winds steadily uphill through thick undergrowth in the shadows of the trees, and at one point crosses a small ravine. It becomes Boucher Trail after crossing Nate Harrison Road.

The high point of the hike (and the park) is Boucher Hill, a popular drive-up site topped by some antennas. From there, on a clear day, you can look west to the blue Pacific and south along the coastal strip into Baja California. To get back to your starting point, you can follow either branch of the narrow, paved road that loops around Boucher Hill, or take a path that runs along the ridge between both branches of that road.

Weir at Pauma Creek

18

Trip 1, Trail 2
Doane Valley Nature Trail

Approximate distance: 1 mile
  for the loop
Elevation at trailhead: 4650 feet
Low point: 4550 feet
High point: 4700 feet

Nowhere else in the county, in my opinion, will you find comparable mountain scenery and atmosphere to match the forests and meadows along Doane Creek. The Doane Valley Nature Trail, a loop through Lower Doane Valley, offers the best in scenic possibilities. An informative trail guide leaflet may be obtained at the trailhead, with descriptions of the wide variety of vegetation you'll find along the trail.

You may find a box containing trail guides in the parking lot next to Doane Pond. The lake is stocked with trout, and is open to fishing year-round. Picnic tables with stoves are here, as well as rest rooms.

Walking downstream along Doane Creek, when it is flowing in a lively manner early in the year, is a genuine delight. Lining the creek are magnificent white fir, incense cedar, box elder and white alder trees, all described in detail by the leaflet. Past a giant incense cedar, you emerge in the meadows of Lower Doane Valley. Late spring and early summer wildflowers dot the rolling expanse of grass, and mature pines, firs and cedars form an imposing wall surrounding it. Lower Doane Trail, branching to the left, will take you to an old weir (dam) on Pauma Creek, if you wish to make the side trip. The nature trail continues back uphill to Doane Valley Campground, which itself is a few hundred yards by paved road from the starting point at Doane Pond.

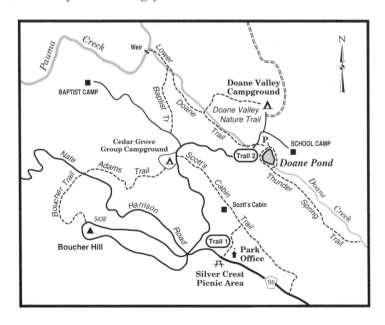

19

Trip 1, Trail 3
Fry Creek Nature Trail

Approximate distance: 1.5 miles
  for the loop
Low point (trailhead): 4930 feet
High point (Penny Pines): 5300 feet

This short walk along the heavily wooded slopes overlooking Fry Creek is most rewarding in late October. The contrasting blue of the sky, the somber green of live oaks and pines, and the yellow, autumnal color of black oaks delight the eye. The fall weather is changeable—warm Indian summer days may alternate with chilly and blustery periods, but clear skies prevail most of the time. A sudden gust may unleash a torrent of falling acorns, and you may see squirrels scurrying around in a last-ditch effort of gathering food for the coming winter.

The main (northern) part of the trail begins at the entrance to Fry Creek Campground, off County Highway S-6, and ends in a Penny Pines plantation at the upper end of the Fry Creek drainage. A lesser-used and poorly maintained (southern) section of the trail loops back to the campground. If you can't find that segment of the trail, simply follow the road that descends from the pines plantation eastward toward the campground.

Acorn cache in pine tree

Trip 1, Trail 4
Observatory Trail

Approximate distance: 2 miles one-way
Low point (Observatory Campground):
 4800 feet
High point (Palomar Observatory):
 5500 feet

As you might expect, the average visitor to Palomar arrives in a car on the paved road, takes in the sights at the observatory, and departs in a like fashion. Not many are aware of the fine trail that roughly parallels the last two miles of road, between the Palomar Observatory entrance and Observatory Campground.

It works well if you can be dropped off at either end, and later be picked up at the opposite end. The ascent to the observatory from the campground involves an 800-foot elevation gain, so if you're not too athletic, try the downhill direction.

Benches are provided at convenient intervals along the trail for those who wish to rest. One resting spot on the trail's lower end looks out over picturesque Mendenhall Valley, which is part of the upper watershed of the San Luis Rey River. Higher up, the trail crosses a number of ravines that come alive as little brooks for a couple of months after heavy rain or snowfall. All the water crossing your path ends up in Lake Henshaw, where it is temporarily stored and then released into the San Luis Rey River along Highway 76.

If you're heading in the up (north) direction, the first sight of the dazzling white 200-inch Hale telescope dome is startling. But you must go inside to get a feeling for the enormous scale of both the building and the instrument inside. The nearby museum has photo-exhibits of astronomical objects taken with the 200-inch and other, smaller telescopes on the mountain. It also contains a scale model of the 200-inch diameter mirror. Visitors are welcome at the museum and inside the glassed-in gallery of the big dome from 8 a.m. to 4 p.m. daily.

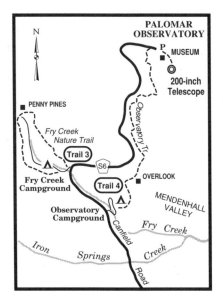

Trip 1, Trail 5
Dripping Springs Trail

Approximate distance: 13 miles
  up and back
Low point (trailhead): 1620 feet
High point (on Agua Tibia ridge):
  4420 feet

Several wilderness areas have been set aside by the Forest Service in Southern California to protect certain areas that have remained in an essentially natural state. Agua Tibia Wilderness in the Palomar Mountains was the first such reserve in San Diego County. Of special interest here were stands of native chaparral that had not been burned for more than a century. Unfortunately, a wildfire devastated most of the Agua Tibia area in 1989, incinerating what used to be a whole forest of "gargantuan" (20-foot-high) manzanita and ribbonwood shrubs. The next decade or two will see the rebirth of the "elfin forest" of mature chaparral on these slopes. In the meantime, the area will be one of the better spots for searching out spring wildflowers, as many kinds of flowers will only germinate following a fire.

While the pine-clad upper elevations of Agua Tibia Mountain are contained in San Diego County, its lower slopes, now draped in a tangled growth of sage and young chaparral plants, extend northward into Riverside County. Dripping Springs Trail begins at Dripping Springs Campground and ascends 2800 feet to the half-singed conifer forest on Agua Tibia Mountain's summit ridge. The round-trip completion of the entire

route in one day can be considered a challenge to all but the most physically fit individuals, but even less-motivated hikers should find the lower end of the trail interesting.

To reach the trailhead from San Diego, drive north on Interstate 15, then head 10 miles east on Highway 79 to Dripping Springs Campground. You'll need a wilderness permit to enter Agua Tibia—even for a day hike, so contact the Cleveland National Forest (788-0250) first to inquire about obtaining one. Permits

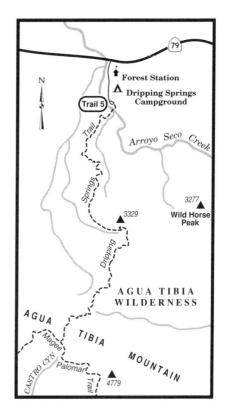

22

are available at the Dripping Springs Forest Station, adjacent to the campground, but only during fire season, which runs from summer into fall. Do inquire about the condition of the Dripping Springs Trail, which varies depending on how much maintenance it has received.

Starting from a small parking area at the south end of Dripping Springs Campground, the trail crosses the boulder-strewn bed of Arroyo Seco Creek, and begins a winding ascent. After a while, Vail Lake, with a backdrop of Southern California's loftiest mountains—San Gorgonio and San Jacinto—comes into view in the north.

The farther you go, the less distinct the trail becomes. Maintenance is infrequent, and the vigorous growth of the fire-following shrubs smothers the trail after every rainy season.

After four miles, the trail descends a little and a view opens up to the southeast. The white dome of the Hale Telescope at Palomar Observatory gleams on a distant ridge. Soon you follow sharp switchbacks again, with the scenery changing from low chaparral to scattered, singed oak and pine trees. At the trail's end is the Magee-Palomar Trail, an abandoned fire road maintained only as a foot trail now. For a fine view of the mountains and valleys to the south and the Pacific Ocean in the west, walk a few hundred feet southeast on the Magee-Palomar Trail to a point overlooking Castro Canyon.

Mountain mahogany chaparral

Backcountry road near Julian

Trip 2
The Julian Area

Facilities and Points of Interest:

Julian Museum (765-0227)
Eagle Mine (765-9921)
William Heise County Park ▲ ⋔
(694-3049)
Inaja Memorial Picnic Ground ⋔
(788-0250)

On the first of March 1870, nine days after the discovery of a gold-bearing quartz ledge in the pine-covered mountains behind San Diego, a shipment of 1200 pounds of rich ore arrived in the city, where one-third of it was dumped into a store window downtown for public exhibition. Crowds gathered and excitement grew by the minute. A horde of would-be prospectors grabbed what implements were available and hastened to stake their own claim to wealth in the mountains. The stampede was on. When they arrived at the gold mines, the hopes of the miners were inflamed by the discovery of a new strike nearby, and another the following day, and yet another ...

In the first month of frantic activity, 260 claims and 40 noteworthy discoveries were made. One miner wrote in the *San Diego Daily Union*: "One scarcely knows whether he is on his head or heels. Imagine 800 men turned loose in the mountains with as little sense and as much 'friskyness' as many wild horses. The people here are positively wild. Such a thing as sober thought is unknown. The rumor comes that Tom, Dick, or Harry has struck it, and forthwith the whole camp rushes pell-mell for the new diggin's. People don't sleep here at all, or if they do, they are more lucky than I."

A mining district was organized and named after Mike S. Julian, a pioneer settler and former Confederate captain. The townsite was hastily laid out and lots surveyed by "stepping them off." By 1872, gold shipments from the Julian-Banner-Wynola area were averaging $9,000 a week, and the Stonewall Mine near Cuyamaca Lake was well on its way to producing an eventual $2,000,000 worth of gold.

Gold mining began to decline in 1874 with the exhaustion of easily milled ore. Big strikes elsewhere were luring miners away, and some men turned to ranching or agriculture. Except for a brief resurgence of activity in the 1890s, the gold rush had ended by the 1880s. The legacy of Julian in the twentieth century had become not that of gold, but of apples and tourism. In 1915, the Julian apple exhibit at the San Francisco World's Fair took the Gold Cup in its class, and today as then the residents of Julian pride themselves on the superior quality of their apples. For many years now, the townspeople have held a series of special events in the fall to celebrate the harvest—or at least bring in extra business from tourists. These convivial gatherings sometimes attract so many visitors from all over Southern California that the town has been literally overwhelmed on past occasions.

Today, the town of Julian, set amid the gentle farmland and forests surrounding it, scarcely betrays the turmoil of its early existence. Tool into town on the two-block-long Main Street, and the old-fashioned storefront façades seem to strike a pose reminiscent of similar sleepy towns in the Mother Lode country of Northern California. Just around the corner is the Julian Museum (open weekends) which contains tools, clothing, home furnishings, and other artifacts of the gold rush days. Nearby you may tour the Eagle Mine, a restored and working gold mine. Drive out C Street, east of town, to reach the entrance.

Seven miles west of Julian, on Highway 78/79, is Santa Ysabel. Long before the arrival of the gold miners, an *asistencia* or sub-mission was established near here by the padres from Mission San Diego to minister to the many Indians who lived in the area. Today, a new chapel stands upon the old site, and continues to serve the Indians of several reservations in the vicinity. Santa Ysabel proper, right at the crossroads of Highways 78 and 79, has become quite a lively tourist stop, with two restaurants and a bakery regionally famous for its "mission bread" and other exotic varieties of baked goods.

To fully capture the country atmosphere of the Julian area, you should drive or bicycle the back roads that ramble over the rolling hills, across the orchards, and through the wooded ravines in back of town. Farmer Road and Wynola Road (north of town); and Pine Hills Road,

Eagle Peak Road, Deer Lake Park Road, and Frisius Drive (south of town) are all excellent for this purpose. William Heise County Park is a great spot to go for a picnic and hiking.

In selecting a route to Julian, San Diegans have a choice between two basic routes, each 60 miles in length. So, for the sake of variety, you might as well make this a loop trip. From San Diego you can proceed east on Interstate 8 to Descanso, then go north on Highway 79 through Cuyamaca Rancho State Park to Julian. Alternately you can travel Highways 78 or 67 through Ramona and continue on Highway 78 through Santa Ysabel to Julian.

While in the Julian area, stop at one of the many friendly roadside markets or restaurants. You might wish to try a cup of hot or ice-cold cider (depending on the season), and purchase some of the locally grown apples to take home with you. In addition, no visit to Julian—at least in recent years—is considered complete without devouring a slice of apple pie.

Glenn's View at Heise Park

26

Trip 2: Julian

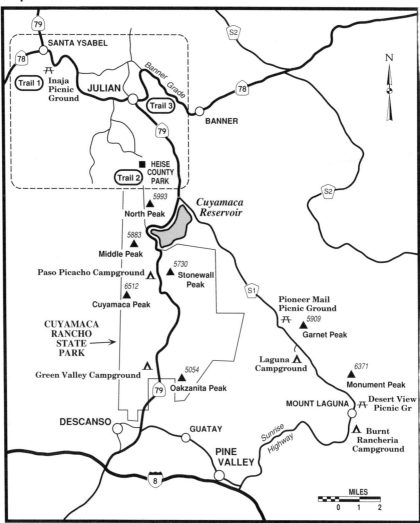

Trip 2, Trail 1
Inaja Trail

Approximate distance: 1 mile
for the loop
Low point (trailhead): 3320 feet
High point: 3440 feet

The Inaja Trail loops around the brow of a ridge just outside Inaja Memorial Picnic Ground, one mile south of Santa Ysabel and six miles west of Julian on Highway 78/79. It is worth a stop here in the morning on your way up to the mountains. At the high point on the trail, you overlook the rugged upper gorge of the San Diego River, which descends southwest toward the coast along a remarkably linear course. Occasionally, on spring and summer mornings, the marine layer of dense low clouds or fog hides all but the tops of the ridges and peaks around you. On the north side of the trail there's quite a different view of the bucolic Santa Ysabel Valley, framed by gentle, oak-studded hills.

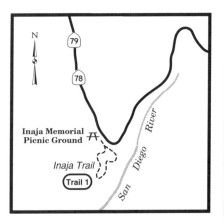

Granite tor along Inaja Trail

28

Trip 2, Trail 2
William Heise County Park

Approximate distances: 1 to 3 miles
  round trip, depending on the route
Low point (trailhead): 4350 feet
Highest point (Glenn's View): 4940 feet

In contrast to most other parks in the extensive San Diego County system, William Heise Park is large enough to support a modest network of hiking trails. Set among majestic live oaks in a secluded valley, it is available for day use at a modest charge. Drive one mile west from Julian to Pine Hills Road, then turn south and follow the signs to the park's entrance off Frisius Road.

Once inside, proceed to the picnic area at the far end of the park to pick up the one-mile, self-guided nature trail. When the nature trail starts looping back to the picnic area, you have a choice of continuing to Glenn's View, on the crest of the ridge to the east. On the way up you'll pass by some fine examples of manzanita

On the trail at Heise Park

shrubs, distinguished by their reddish, sometimes peeling bark. Once on the top of the ridge, there's a long view down the rounded spine of the Laguna Mountains, and across a slice of brown desert floor below and to the east. You can return either the way you came, or take a longer, alternative route along the Desert Overlook Trail.

Another good, short hike in the park, the Cedar Trail, takes you past a seasonal pond and up along a slope clad in aromatic incense cedars. It begins at a camping area on the right, about one-half mile beyond the park's entrance.

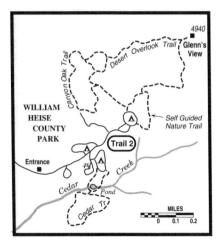

29

Warlock Mine

Trip 2, Trail 3
Old Banner Grade

Approximate distance: 3 miles
 down and back
Low point (Warlock Mine): 3460 feet
High point (trailhead): 4160 feet

Serious gold mining in San Diego County has all but ceased, but traces of the old mining efforts remain. For a look at some of the more recently abandoned prospects around Julian, take a walk down the Old Banner Grade.

Drive about one mile east of Julian on Highway 78, then make a right turn at Whispering Pines Drive. Immediately after, make another sharp right to connect with Woodland Road. One half mile beyond, take the left fork. Park where you can, taking care to block the road. From there you can proceed on foot on what was originally the Banner Grade.

Down below is the modern road through Banner Canyon—Highway 78. It appears only slightly less twisting than the old road, and offers a more gradual, if longer, descent toward Banner in the valley below. Abandoned mine shafts pierce the earth on the steep slopes above and below you, but many of them are now well concealed by thick brush. The Warlock Mine, including the decrepit traces of a processing mill, comes into view about one mile down. It last operated in the 1950s. Take care when poking around the ruins, and don't enter any of the mine tunnels.

Beyond the Warlock Mine, Old Banner Grade runs into private property, so it is best to turn back. Your return trip, which gains some 700 feet of elevation, will take considerably longer than the deceptively easy descent.

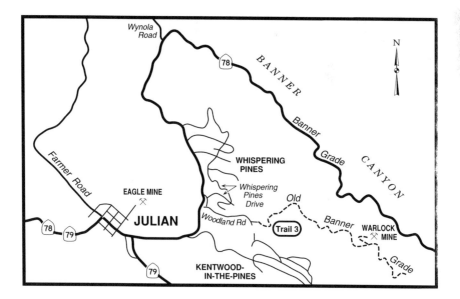

31

Dry lake bed—Cuyamaca Reservoir

Trip 3
The Cuyamaca Mountains

Facilities and Points of Interest:
(for additional information about all,
phone 765-0755)

Indian exhibit at Cuyamaca Rancho State
Park headquarters

Natural history exhibit at Paso Picacho

Stonewall Mine site

Paso Picacho Λ ⋔

Green Valley Λ ⋔

Now that suburban growth has spread into the community of Alpine, only about 10 miles away by crow's flight, the Cuyamaca Mountains aren't what you could call remote anymore. Still, their mile-high altitude, rich vegetation, clean air, and four-season climate keep them quite distinct from the foothills and flatlands below.

Luckily, most of the Cuyamaca range falls within Cuyamaca Rancho State Park. It remains unavailable for development, but very available for picnicking, hiking, horse riding, camping, mountain biking (along some but not all trails), and other passive recreational uses. With easy access by way of freeway and two-lane highway, the park attracts hundreds of thousands of visitors yearly, the vast majority of whom are San Diegans or Southern Californians out for just the day.

The Cuyamaca Mountains have, in fact, long been a favorite of Southern California inhabitants. As early as 7000 years ago and until as recently as the gold boom of the last century, the Cuyamacas were a summer residence of the Kumeyaay Indians. The name Cuyamaca derives from a Spanish version of the Indian word meaning approximately "the place where it rains."

In 1845, most of the present park area was incorporated into Rancho Cuyamaca by the Mexican government, and subsequently it changed hands several times until its eventual purchase by the State of California in 1933.

Every season in the Cuyamacas has its own attraction. Summers tend to be hot in the daytime, but refreshingly cool in the early morning when the low-angle sun stabs across the transparent air and delineates the gentle contours of the landscape. Summer thundershowers, caused by moist air moving in from the southeast, temper some of the hottest days and bring out earthy aromas from the chaparral and forest.

Fall brings displays of fine autumn color—mostly in the yellowing leaves of the black oak—which peaks in late October and early November. Dry Santa Ana winds can rake the area anytime from late September through the winter, clearing away all trace of haze or smog at the higher elevations and leaving behind crystalline air and phenomenal visibility in all directions except over the coastline.

During an average winter, one or two cold Pacific storms have enough punch to dump a foot or two of snow on the higher Cuyamaca peaks. After these storms pass on, cold, dry north winds sometimes usher in periods of exceptional atmospheric clarity from sea level up. During these times, even the western vistas sometime become haze-free, and your gaze can take in the Pacific Ocean dimpled by Santa Catalina Island, San Clemente Island, and Mexico's Coronado Islands.

As for the virtues of spring in the Cuyamacas: they really need not be elaborated—anyone who has lived in a climate with four well-defined seasons will understand.

The diversity of terrain and plant life in the Cuyamaca Mountains and beyond supports an abundance of wildlife. One example of this is the wide variety of birds found here. Located midway between the coast and desert, the area attracts birds from both coastal and desert habitats. For more on birds and other wildlife, visit the natural history exhibit at the entrance of Paso Picacho Campground.

Tranquillity may be found in the Cuyamacas, off the highway, on more than 100 miles of hiking and equestrian trails within the park. Two primitive camps for backpackers, Arroyo Seco and Granite Springs, are located near the outer boundaries; and two equestrian facilities are in park's north end. No trail strays more than a few miles from the highway that bisects the park, so all are well suited for one-day exploration.

From downtown San Diego, the Cuyamaca Mountains are barely an hour away via Interstate 8. Simply drive east on I-8, and take the Highway 79 exit north. Once on 79, in the Descanso valley, two prominent

Cuyamaca features come into view: Cuyamaca Peak has a dark, rounded summit—the highest point within 30 miles. Stonewall Peak, to the right (east) of Cuyamaca Peak, is nearly 1000 feet lower, but its pointed summit with an exposed patch of granite on the south side distinguishes it from other summits in the area.

There are several turnouts on Highway 79 once you pass into the park. Free parking is allowed in the turnouts, but time restrictions apply in some. Overnight parking is prohibited, except inside the campgrounds, where a fee is charged whether you camp or not. Day-use and camping fees have greatly increased over the past decade, but they go a long way toward maintaining the park for your enjoyment.

Green Valley Campground lies on the left, nestled amid the oak woodland that accompanies the Sweetwater River. Popular Green Valley Falls lies near its south end— get there early (on the weekends) if you want to nab a spot in the nearby parking lot. Depending on the amount of recent rain, the normally placid cascades here can sometimes turn into a maelstrom of rushing water and spray. It is by far the most easily accessible waterfall in San Diego having the potential of being spectacular in flood conditions.

Beyond Green Valley Campground, Highway 79 rolls on through the grassy meadows of Green Valley. You pass the turnoff for the park headquarters and Indian Museum, which are housed in a rustic stone home that belonged to the last private owners of the Cuyamaca Rancho

in the '20s and early '30s. On beyond, the oaks and pines thicken alongside the roadway, and tight twists and turns necessitate speeds as slow as 15 miles per hour.

Highway 79 comes to a crest at Paso Picacho Campground, which is located atop the saddle connecting Stonewall and Cuyamaca peaks. Two of the most popular trails in the park start here and climb with no hesitation to the two flanking summits (Trails 5 and 6 in this section).

As you near the north end of the park, a paved road branches right. It provides access to the equestrian campgrounds and to the site of the Stonewall Mine near Cuyamaca Reservoir. The mine was the most productive of those active during the Julian gold boom. Nearby, the good-sized town of Cuyamaca had grown up to serve the sudden influx of population.

Leaving the park, Highway 79 encircles Cuyamaca Reservoir and finally heads north to Julian. The lake level fluctuates greatly depending on the season and whether the year has been a wet or a dry one. There are a couple of cafes near the lake shore, and you can rent a boat or fish on the lake.

When returning to San Diego, you might consider the route north through Julian. Simply continue north on Highway 79 to Julian, then go west on Highway 78 through Santa Ysabel. At Ramona, Highway 78 continues toward Escondido and Oceanside, while Highway 67 runs south to El Cajon and San Diego.

Winter oaks, Paso Picacho

Trip 3: Cuyamaca Mountains

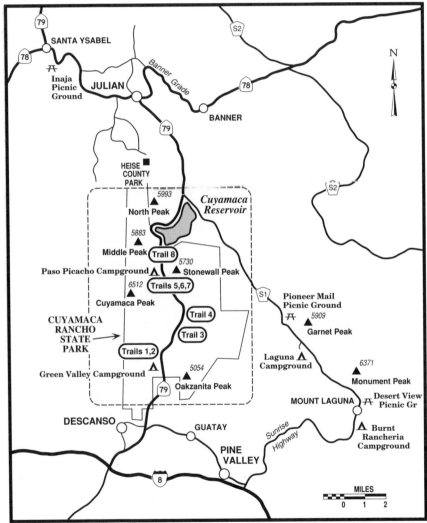

Trip 3, Trail 1
Green Valley Falls-
Pine Ridge Trail

Approximate distance: 4 miles
 for the loop
Low point (Green Valley Falls):
 3850 feet
High point (Pine Ridge): 4400 feet

Green Valley Campground is set among magnificent canyon live oaks near the lower end of Green Valley, where the Sweetwater River narrows and finally cascades over a series of huge boulders. This (the Falls Picnic Area at the campground's south end) is the starting point for our hike through Cuyamaca's foothill chaparral zone.

Head south on the fire road/trail leading toward Green Valley Falls, lying to the left down a short side trail. After visiting the falls, continue on the fire road, which parallels the pine- and oak-shaded Sweetwater River in the downstream direction. At the next intersection turn right and follow South Boundary Fire Road uphill to the California Riding and Hiking Trail. You're in chaparral now—unpleasant, shadeless terrain on a hot summer day, but softer looking and fragrant in cooler weather. Go north on the Riding and Hiking Trail for just over a mile to Pine Ridge Trail, on the right. The sign here indicates 1.5 miles to Green Valley Campground. The trail slashes upward through a veritable forest of manzanita toward the crest of Pine Ridge, then meanders downward toward the edge of the campground.

From atop the ridge there's a terrific view encompassing the length of Green Valley and the course of the Sweetwater River.

Green Valley Falls

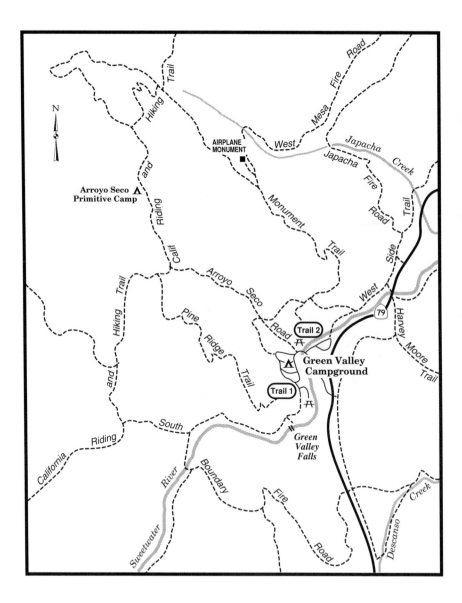

N

AIRPLANE MONUMENT

Arroyo Seco Primitive Camp

Hiking

and

Riding

Calif

Hiking

Trail

and

Riding

California

Pine

Ridge

Trail

South

Arroyo

Seco

Road

West

Mesa

Fire

Road

Japacha

Japacha

Fire

Road

Creek

Side

Trail

Monument

Trail

West

79

Harvey

Moore

Trail

Trail 2

Green Valley
Campground

Trail 1

Green
Valley
Falls

River

Boundary

Fire

Sweetwater

Road

Descanso

Creek

Trip 3, Trail 2
Airplane Ridge-
Monument Trail

Approximate distance: 3 miles
 up and back
Low point (trailhead): 3960 feet
High point (Airplane Monument):
 4770 feet

The Monument Trail is a short, easy walk from Green Valley Campground to the monument on Airplane Ridge. The trail begins at a day-use parking and picnic area on the north end of the campground. After rising on a chaparral-covered slope overlooking Green Valley, it joins a wider trail—West Mesa Fire Road. Go straight ahead for about 100 yards, and follow the narrower Monument Trail as it splits off to the left.

The appearance of an airplane engine in the middle of the path is an incongruous sight, but a plaque set here explains the details: "In Memory of Col. F. C. Marshall and 1st Lt. C. L. Webber who fell at this spot Dec. 7, 1922." From the end of the trail, you can look upon the densely wooded Japacha Creek canyon below and up to the cone-shaped profile of Stonewall Peak in the distance.

Airplane monument

Trip 3, Trail 3
Dyar Spring Trail

Approximate distance: 5.5 miles
 for the loop
Low point (trailhead): 4000 feet
High point (East Mesa): 4760 feet

This loop through terrain typical of the lower elevations and drier portions of the Cuyamaca Mountains includes a stop midway at Dyar Spring, a year-round source of good drinking water. You can conveniently pick up the trail at the large turnout/parking area next to the Sweetwater River bridge on Highway 79, where all-day parking is allowed.

From the parking area take the Harvey Moore Trail, a designated equestrian trail. Two miles ahead, Dyar Spring Trail intersects on the left. The open, grassy expanse now before you is known as East Mesa. Early or late in day, you can sit quietly under a tree at the meadow's edge and watch for mule deer and coyotes.

After going about a mile north on Dyar Spring Fire Road, you come to Dyar Spring, where water gushes from a pipe on the left. You can fill your water bottle here, and dash some water across your face and body if the day is a hot one.

Back on the trail again, continue north across tall grass and into the chaparral. The rocky path continues up and over a low ridge, then goes down sharply to the junction of Juaquapin Trail on a wooded saddle. Go left on Juaquapin Trail, following the grassy banks of Juaquapin Creek.

Near the junction of the trail that leads south to the Harvey Moore Trail, look under the nearby grove of live oaks and discover several Indian mortar holes. This is one of many such places in the Cuyamaca Mountains where the Kumeyaay Indians used to grind up acorns for making a nutritious meal.

At the junction of that south-going trail, you can either go south, back to Harvey Moore Trail, or stay right and go left at the next junction to return to the Sweetwater River bridge by way of East Side Trail.

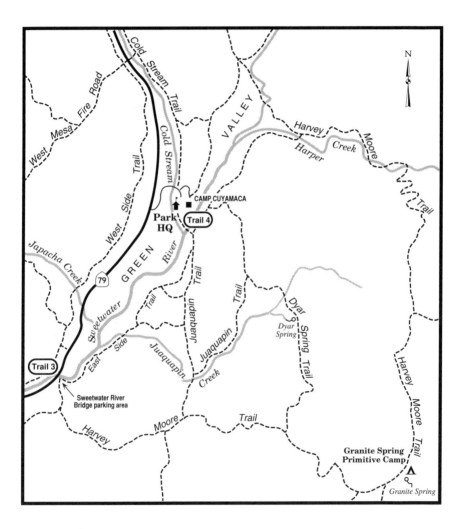

N

Cold Stream Trail

West Mesa Fire Road

West

West Side Trail

Cold Stream

Cold Stream

VALLEY

Harvey

Harper

Creek

Moore

Trail

CAMP CUYAMACA

Park HQ

Trail 4

GREEN

River

Japacha Creek

79

Sweetwater

Juaquapin Trail

Juaquapin Trail

Dyar Spring

Dyar Spring

Dyar Spring Trail

Trail 3

East Side

Juaquapin

Juaquapin Creek

Sweetwater River Bridge parking area

Harvey

Moore

Trail

Harvey Moore Trail

Granite Spring Primitive Camp

Granite Spring

Trip 3, Trail 4
Harper Creek

Approximate distance: 3 miles
out and back
Low point (Sweetwater River): 4050 feet
High point: 4340 feet

The beautiful Harper Creek canyon, on the east side of Green Valley, is a seldom-visited but unique area of the park. This gorge, cut by a tributary of the Sweetwater River, contains some fascinating examples of water-polished rock. Harper Creek is a lively little brook from the first substantial rains of autumn or winter until it is sucked dry by midsummer's heat. Occasionally, a late summer thunderstorm will revive the stream for a few days or weeks. During early winter, sunlight seldom penetrates to the bottom of the canyon, so you'll want to be careful of slippery ice.

The fastest and most direct way to reach the canyon is by starting at the park headquarters area in Green Valley, where you can park your car for up to 2 hours. Start by walking eastward toward the Sweetwater River. The facilities along the bank of the river—classrooms, playing fields, and a swimming pool—are part of Camp Cuyamaca, a San Diego city and county school camp.

Find a place to cross the usually shallow river and take the path (East Side Trail) leading north alongside the river and across Green Valley. When you arrive at the mouth of Harper Creek canyon, about a mile from the start, you can boulder-hop up-canyon along the bottom if the water is low or absent—or otherwise wade through. Water-polished rock tends to be slippery when wet, so proceed with caution.

About a half-mile up, the exposed rock disappears and the canyon becomes choked with vegetation. This is a good place to turn back. On the bank to the left you may see the Harvey Moore Trail, which you can follow back to the mouth of the canyon if you've had enough boulder-hopping.

Harper Creek

View east from Stonewall Peak

Trip 3, Trail 5
Stonewall Peak Trail

Approximate distance: 4 miles
 out and back to Stonewall Peak;
 5.5 miles for the loop through
 Los Caballos Camp
Elevation at trailhead: 4870 feet
High point (Stonewall Peak): 5730 feet
Low point (Los Caballos Camp): 4720 feet

The many-switchbacked Stonewall Peak Trail along the peak's west side gains nearly 1000 feet in two miles; but it's not a difficult route, even for the novice hiker. My three-year-old once made it all the way up and back, with some help and lots of patience on my part.

About halfway up the trail, a broad panorama of the Cuyamacas begins to unfold. Cuyamaca Reservoir, to the north, is probably the most striking feature. During a wet winter, the entire reservoir fills, but much of the time the uncovered, upper, shallow end becomes a meadow used for grazing cattle.

The trees start thinning near the top, as you reach a T-intersection. Turn right and shortly after arrive at the base of Stonewall's imposing summit block of granitic rock. A guard rail and steps cut into the granite make the climb to the fenced viewpoint at the top easy. (If you have small children, though, they must be guided with a firm grip.)

The view at the top encompasses the entire Cuyamaca and Laguna Mountain region, although distant views in the east and west directions are cut off by foreground ranges. You can easily identify the rounded peaks of the main Cuyamaca range: from north to south they are North Peak, Middle Peak, Cuyamaca Peak, and Japacha Peak. Highway 79 appears as a gray ribbon with toylike cars on it running from Cuyamaca Reservoir on the north, across the Paso Picacho saddle and down into Green Valley in the south.

If you want to return to Paso Picacho Campground by a longer route, retrace your steps a few hundred feet down the Stonewall Peak Trail. From there, another branch of the trail goes northward toward the equestrian campgrounds. Steep and rocky at first, it skirts Little Stonewall Peak and then descends more gradually to meet the California Riding and Hiking Trail near Los Caballos Camp. Turn left and head toward Highway 79. Remain on the same (east) side of Highway 79 when the Riding and Hiking Trail forks west, and continue on a gradually uphill course back to Paso Picacho Campground.

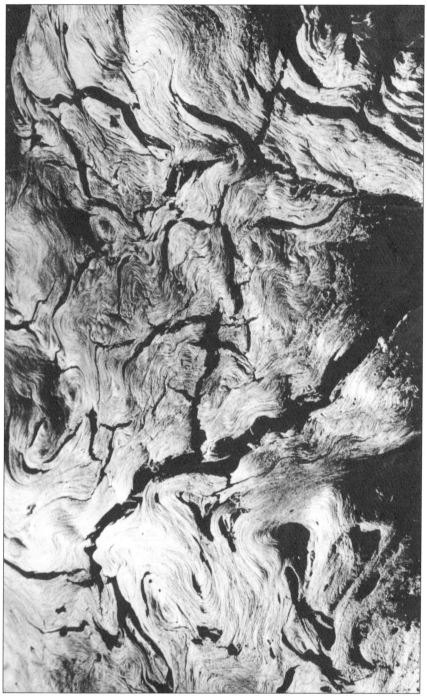

Nature's artistry

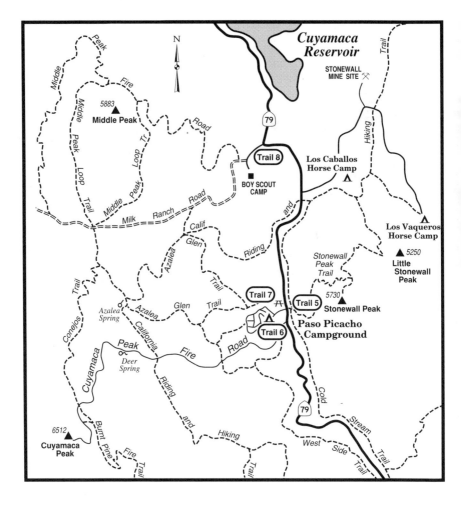

Cuyamaca
Reservoir

STONEWALL
MINE SITE

Middle Peak

5883
Middle Peak

Fire

Road

Peak

Peak Loop Trail

Middle Peak Loop Tr.

Milk   Ranch   Road

Trail 8

BOY SCOUT
CAMP

Los Caballos
Horse Camp

Hiking

Trail

79

Riding   and

Los Vaqueros
Horse Camp

5250
Little
Stonewall
Peak

Calif

Glen

Azalea

Glen

Trail

Riding

Stonewall
Peak
Trail

Trail 7

Trail 5

5730
Stonewall Peak

Azalea
Spring

Conejos   Trail

Cuyamaca   Peak

Azalea   Glen   Trail

California

Deer
Spring

Fire   Road

Trail 6

Paso Picacho
Campground

6512
Cuyamaca
Peak

Burnt Pine

Riding   and

Fire   Trail

Hiking

Trail

79

Cold

West   Side   Trail

Stream   Trail

N

47

Trip 3, Trail 6
Cuyamaca Peak

Approximate distance: 5.5 miles
 up and back
Low point (trailhead): 4870 feet
High point (Cuyamaca Peak): 6512 feet

The Cuyamaca Peak Fire Road (a.k.a. the Lookout Road) begins at the fire station adjacent to Paso Picacho Campground and winds steadily uphill to the summit of Cuyamaca Peak—the second highest point in San Diego County. The road is paved all the way, one-lane wide, and closed to unauthorized vehicles. You can start right at Highway 79, or get access to it by means of walking through the south end of the campground.

The going is rather easy at first as the trail gently twists and turns through a nice collection of black oaks. Look behind you to see the rocky summit of Stonewall Peak standing tall through the trees. After crossing the California Riding and Hiking Trail just over a mile from the campground, the trail steepens considerably, and Jeffrey pines, incense-cedars, and white firs grow in greater numbers. Much of this upper-elevation forest was devastated by wildfires in 1950 and 1970. While still recovering almost 40 years later, it was hit by a series of drought years that lasted from the mid 1980s to the early '90s. If plenty of rain continues through the mid-'90s, the forest will quickly bounce back to its former glory.

Beyond Deer Spring, which is currently boxed in and unavailable for drinking purposes, the road turns south and the view expands to include Cuyamaca Reservoir and the various ranges of the Anza-Borrego Desert beyond it.

Near the top, Burnt Pine Fire Trail forks to the left. With a final burst of energy, you reach Cuyamaca's antenna-bewhiskered summit. It's easy to see why a fire lookout tower was, until recently, located here. The view is the most comprehensive in San Diego County. Look north to see Palomar Observatory's 200-inch telescope dome gleaming on the dark Palomar ridge 30 miles to the north. San Diego and the Pacific Ocean lie in the west, haze permitting. In the south, a succession of ever-distant ridges marches deep into Baja California. The desert view in the east is somewhat blocked by the Laguna Mountains, although on clear days the Salton Sea can be seen to the northeast. One of the unassuming ridges to the north has a bump called Hot Springs Mountain—which, at 6533 feet, barely qualifies as San Diego County's highest point.

Far below you is your starting point at Paso Picacho Campground, and beyond that our old friend, Stonewall Peak, which has now shrunk to a mere dimple on the landscape. Returning to Paso Picacho, you can watch Stonewall loom larger against the sky, eventually attaining its former glory as your perspective changes.

Southeast of Cuyamaca Peak, the rare Cuyamaca cypress has established a foothold within its sole native habitat on the steep slopes of the headwaters of King Creek. It, too, was nearly wiped out by the fires, but has recovered nicely. Like some varieties of pine trees, these cypress trees readily germinate and sprout like weeds on ashen soil in the aftermath of a hot fire.

As an alternate way of returning—instead of taking the paved road all the way back, you might want to detour north on the California Riding and Hiking Trail. There you can visit Azalea Spring, which has water available for drinking, and then follow Azalea Glen Trail back to your starting point.

Trip 3, Trail 7
Azalea Glen Trail

Approximate distance: 3 miles
  for the loop
Low point (trailhead): 4850 feet
High point (Azalea Spring): 5370 feet

Hiking the Azalea Glen Trail is ideal for those who wish to enjoy an hour or two of the best Cuyamaca scenery—indeed, some of the finest scenery Southern California has to offer. Special attractions are found in every season along this trail: wildflowers spreading over the meadows in the spring, welcome shade in the summertime, crisp weather and autumn color in the fall, and occasional frostings of snow in winter.

The well-marked trail begins at Paso Picacho, just across the parking lot from the picnic area at the north end. For the most part the path travels through the mixed pine, fir, cedar, and oak forest which is typical of this area, but occasionally you'll run into open meadows. A short dis-tance from the start, the trail divides two ways. If you take the right fork, you'll soon pass through a meadow with a few Indian mortar holes on a granite slab right along the trail.

Azalea Glen Trail joins the California Riding and Hiking Trail about one mile from the campground. From there, you go sharply uphill accompanied by a small stream informally known as Azalea Creek. Watch for the blooming western azalea down along the stream in late spring.

Azalea Spring, dispensing clear, cold water, lies at the top of the uphill stretch. The remainder of Azalea Glen Trail takes you more directly back to Paso Picacho Campground, downhill all the way.

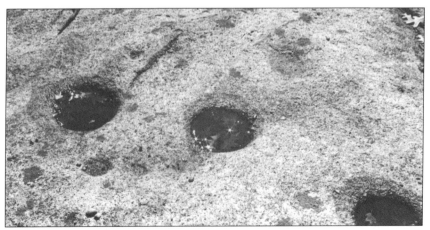

Bedrock mortars, Azalea Glen Trail

Trip 3, Trail 8
Middle Peak

Approximate distance: 5.5 miles
 for the loop
Low point (trailhead): 4660 feet
High point: 5710 feet

Little else distinguishes Middle Peak from neighboring mountains in the main Cuyamaca range other than its exceptionally well-forested upper slopes. Unlike the Cuyamaca and North Peak summits, Middle Peak has not suffered seriously in recent times from the effects of forest fires. Lovers of the deep, dark forest will really like it up there. There are few places in Southern California like this where you can easily lose your sense of direction in broad daylight.

Middle Peak is a low-profile, roughly cone-shaped mountain overlooking Cuyamaca Reservoir to the east. The loop described here begins at a parking turnout on the east side of Highway 79, opposite the intersection of Milk Ranch Road. Follow Milk Ranch Road a few hundred yards, then veer right on Middle Peak Fire Road. Long, lazy zigzags take you from the oak woodland of the lower slope up into a zone of giant incense-cedar, Jeffrey pine, and sugar pine. When you reach Middle Peak Loop Trail, stay right. In a short while you'll reach the 5710-foot high point of the trail. No designated path leads to Middle Peak's summit from here, but you can scramble up if you want to. Don't expect much of a view from the top, as there's dense vegetation on all sides.

Follow Middle Peak Loop Trail as it contours around the north side of the mountain, and remain left on the loop trail as you reach another junction with Middle Peak Fire Road. For a mile you descend the west and south slopes, catching occasional broad views toward the coast, and finally reach Milk Ranch Road. Follow that road back to your starting point, gently downhill all the way.

Sugar pine bark

Trip 4
The Laguna Mountains

Facilities and Points of Interest:
(for additional information about all,
  phone 445-6235)

Laguna Mountain Recreation Area
  Visitor Information Office

Laguna Campground ▲ ⊼

Burnt Rancheria Campground ▲ ⊼

Pioneer Mail Picnic Area ⊼

Desert View Picnic Area ⊼

Mount Laguna Observatory (open-house
  for sky viewing on summer weekends
  by reservation only)

Desert-bordering mountain ranges are not uncommon in Southern California, but their surprising contrasts inspire wonder in the multitudes of visitors who explore them each year. Of these ranges, the Laguna Mountains are the most easily accessible to San Diegans. The pine-crested slopes of these mountains wring out most of the remaining precipitation from moisture-laden coastal clouds moving inland from the Pacific Ocean. Only a meager amount is spared for the Colorado Desert, which lies in a "rain shadow" to the east. The Anza-Borrego Desert State Park, at the foot of the Lagunas, occupies nearly a thousand square miles of this rugged desert.

The majority of the land in the Laguna Mountains is administered by the Cleveland National Forest, although some pockets of privately owned property are here, too. The Forest Service has developed some fine facilities in the Laguna Mountain Recreation Area, high atop the mountain, to accommodate the large number of visitors. In addition to camping and picnicking, evening campfire lecture programs, conducted by rangers or volunteer naturalists, highlight weekend evenings during the summer.

The Laguna Mountains are considered an excellent dark-sky observing site for astronomical research, a distinction shared with Palomar. For this reason, San Diego State University has located its observatory here. A visitor program at the observatory is operated in conjunction with the Forest Service on weekend evenings during the summer.

Many short and long trails in the Laguna Mountain Recreation Area permit detailed exploration of the region. This book (and our map) includes six of these, suitable for short hikes, and also the Pacific Crest Trail, which parallels the mountain escarpment and gives access to several good viewpoints overlooking the desert below.

From San Diego, the Laguna high country lies only a scant hour away by car. The drive is almost a classic opportunity to observe a wide cross-section of terrain and vegetation across San Diego County. As you gradually escape the urban sprawl on Interstate 8 east of El Cajon, the remaining undeveloped hillsides are clothed in an elfin forest of chaparral—less poetically known as scrub brush. Stop at the small rest area and

Trip 4: Laguna Mountains

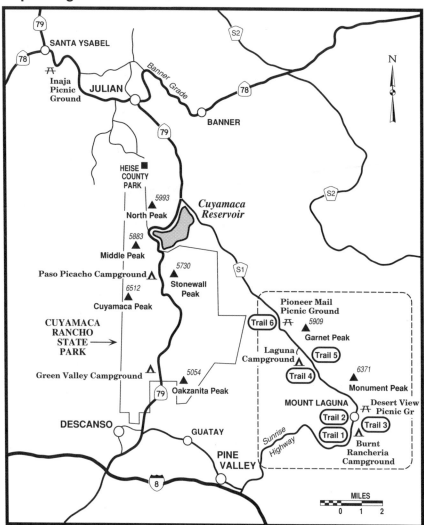

viewpoint on I-8 past Alpine to appreciate how steadfastly this kind of vegetation clings to the rocky slopes. Chaparral begins to give way to scattered oaks and pines at the nearly 4000-foot elevation of Pine Valley. Sunrise Highway (County S-l), the next exit after Pine Valley, is your gateway to the higher Lagunas.

Sunrise Highway first snakes along dry Scove Canyon, but after a few miles, there's a sudden change of character: oaks and pines dominate the landscape after you come around a bend. The temperature drops perceptibly. Past Crouch Meadow, you're back in the forest again as Jeffrey pines stand like sentinels on both sides of the road.

Ahead, Sunrise Highway starts leveling out and passes Burnt Rancheria Campground and the little commercial center of Mount Laguna, with a restaurant, general store, and cabins for rent. Don't miss a stop at the Forest Service Visitor Information Office on the left.

On a bit farther, the access road to the Desert View Picnic Area intersects on your right. Now the highway turns northwest. Again on the right, a spur road leads one-quarter mile to the Vista Point on the slope of Stephenson Peak. On top of the peak are the strange-looking domes of a decommissioned Air Force radar station.

Straight ahead on Sunrise Highway you'll pass the entrance to Laguna Campground and Pioneer Mail Picnic Ground, three and six miles, respectively, from Mount Laguna.

For a slightly longer, but scenic return to San Diego, continue driving northwest on Sunrise Highway past Pioneer Mail Picnic Ground. Several good views of the desert may be had from the road, but pull off on the spur road to Kwaaymii Point (one mile north of Pioneer Mail Picnic Area) for an even more inclusive view.

When you finally arrive at Highway 79 near Cuyamaca Reservoir, you can either turn south through the Cuyamaca Mountains and rejoin Interstate 8 near Descanso, or you may turn north toward Julian. From Julian, Highway 78 leads west toward the coast.

Trip 4, Trail 1
Wooded Hill Nature Trail

Approximate distance: 1.5 miles
 for the loop
Low point (trailhead): 5960 feet
High point (Wooded Hill): 6223 feet

The Wooded Hill Trail is one of three self-guided nature trails in the Laguna Mountain Recreation Area. It's a good one to start with if you wish to become familiar with the native flora and fauna.

The trailhead is on Wooded Hill Road, which intersects Sunrise Highway about two miles southwest of the village of Mount Laguna. You may find a box containing trail-guide leaflets at the start of the trail, or you can pick one up at the Visitor Information Office.

Jeffrey pine, black oak, incense cedar, and several varieties of common chaparral plants are highlighted in the trail guide. In addition to learning about the vegetation, this is a good area to listen for and observe wildlife. Gray squirrels flit about the branches and underbrush, while acorn woodpeckers are busy chipping holes into the trunks of pine trees for acorn storage.

The trail winds up to the top of the appropriately named Wooded Hill, where a direction-finder points out major peaks along the horizon. On exceptionally clear days, the San Diego coastline and the Pacific Ocean sprawl before you. Look for Point Loma, a southward pointing finger jutting into the ocean. On a nearby ridge to the south, you may spot the domes of the Mount Laguna Observatory.

Trip 4, Trail 2
Kwaaymii Trail

Approximate distance: 0.5 mile
 for the loop
Low point (trailhead): 5920 feet
High point: 6020 feet

This short, self-guided nature trail begins right behind the Visitor Information Office in Mount Laguna. It encircles a small hill, known as Pinon Point, then loops back down to the starting point.

Until the present century, the Laguna Mountains were a summer home to bands of Kumeyaay Indians, specifically a sub-tribe known as the Kwaaymii. The trail-guide leaflet explains the Indians' use of native shrubs and trees for food, shelter, clothing, medicinal and ceremonial uses. The Indians were apparently able to live adequately on the natural yield of many different types of vegetation, while supplementing their diet with small game. It is interesting to note that these early natives not only were familiar with the basic concepts of ecology, but also put into practice conservation of natural resources in their everyday lives. As an example, while gathering acorns, the Indian women would leave a certain number behind to insure future generations of oak trees.

A site at the top of the hill was used for processing of acorns. Bedrock mortars (deep holes) and metates (shallow depressions) may be seen along the trail. Acorns were pounded into meal in these grinding holes as the first step in the production of edible food such as soup, pudding, or bread.

On the Kwaaymii Trail

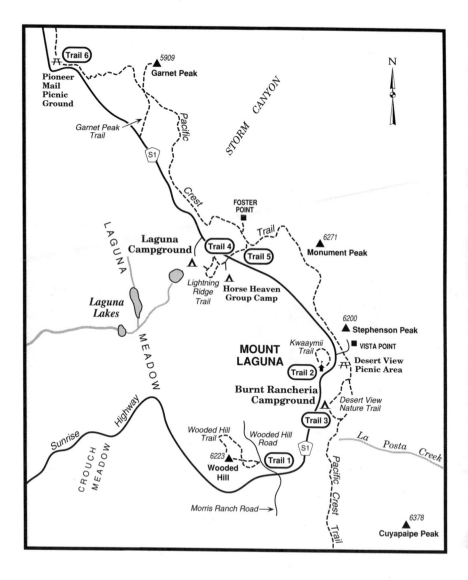

N

Trail 6

5909
Garnet Peak

Pioneer
Mail
Picnic
Ground

Garnet Peak
Trail

Pacific

STORM CANYON

S1

Crest

FOSTER
POINT

Trail

Laguna
Campground

Trail 4

Trail 5

6271
Monument Peak

LAGUNA

Lightning
Ridge
Trail

Horse Heaven
Group Camp

Laguna
Lakes

6200
Stephenson Peak

VISTA POINT

MEADOW

Kwaaymii
Trail

MOUNT
LAGUNA

Desert View
Picnic Area

Trail 2

Burnt Rancheria
Campground

Trail 3

Desert View
Nature Trail

Sunrise

Highway

Wooded Hill
Trail

Wooded Hill
Road

Trail 1

La

Posta

Creek

CROUCH

MEADOW

6223
Wooded
Hill

S1

Morris Ranch Road →

Pacific

Crest

Trail

6378
Cuyapaipe Peak

Trip 4, Trail 3
Desert View Nature Trail

Approximate distance: 1.3 miles
for the loop
Low point (trailhead): 5930 feet
High point: 6050 feet

A parking area has been set aside in Burnt Rancheria Campground for users of the Desert View Nature Trail. Inquire at the Visitor Information Office about the interpretive leaflet for the trail. For a while the trail joins a segment of the Pacific Crest Trail, and where it passes near the campground it may be hard to follow, as people have cut paths to individual campsites.

There are two vistas along the way: the first overlooks the canyon of La Posta Creek, and the second provides a good slice of the Colorado Desert, with southern Anza-Borrego in the foreground.

Lupine

Trip 4, Trail 4
Lightning Ridge Trail

Approximate distance: 1 mile
 for the loop
Low point (trailhead): 5570 feet
High point (Lightning Ridge): 5800 feet

You can approach this rambling trail either from the amphitheater at Laguna Campground, or from the access road off Sunrise Highway into Horse Heaven Group Camp. Again, this is one that may be hard to follow because of the false trails made by people making shortcuts.

Whatever path you take up Lightning Ridge, you're sure to end up at a water tank called Chula Vista Res-

ervoir. From there, you can look down upon Laguna Meadow and the Laguna Lakes. (*Laguna* is the Spanish word for "lake.") Like all natural lakes in San Diego County's mountains, these are ephemeral, brimming with water in winter and spring, but dried out by summer. If the late summer thundershowers have been frequent enough, the lakes will partially fill again.

Laguna Meadow

Trip 4, Trail 5
Foster Point

Approximate distance: 1 mile
 out and back
Low point (trailhead): 5640 feet
High point (Foster Point): 5740 feet

A good view of the Colorado Desert through Storm Canyon is the main attraction of this brief off-the-road excursion. Drive two miles northwest of Mount Laguna to the entrance to Horse Heaven Group Campground. Find a place to park off the pavement.

Begin walking east on the dim traces of a former road/trail across pine-dotted Flathead Flats. After about one-quarter mile, the faint path turns north and approaches a well-defined footpath—the Pacific Crest Trail. Follow the PCT to where it breaks out of the trees and enters the chaparral. Then, a short distance further, take the trail intersecting on the right to Foster Point. You wind another few hundred feet through the brush, and come up to Foster Point, so named for one of the founders of the Sierra Club's San Diego Chapter. The metal direction-finder allows clear sightings and gives distances to many near and far landmarks. The farthest is Southern California's highest mountain, San Gorgonio, in the San Bernardino Mountains. Clear, crisp winter days are best for viewing the distant peaks, but even on a hazy day the drop-off into the desert below is spectacular.

Foster Point monument

60

Trip 4, Trail 7
Garnet Peak

Approximate distance: 4.5 miles
out and back
Low point (trailhead): 5250 feet
High point (Garnet Peak): 5909 feet

Of the many desert view points afforded by road or trail in the Laguna Mountains, my favorite is Garnet Peak. The most interesting, if not quite the shortest, route to the top starts at Pioneer Mail Picnic Ground and uses a portion of the Pacific Crest Trail. Pioneer Mail Picnic Ground is immediately off Sunrise Highway about six miles northwest of the village of Mount Laguna.

While driving toward the picnic ground from Mount Laguna, you (or at least your passengers) get a startling glimpse of the desert to the east. Garnet Peak is visible from there, too, looking more like the edge of a precipice than a peak. A marker at the pine- and oak-shaded picnic area commemorates the "Jackass Mail"— the first transcontinental mail route from Texas to San Diego, named for the pack animals used to haul mail along parts of the route.

From the picnic ground entrance, follow the PCT southeast, paralleling the Sunrise Highway. Soon, the trail turns away from the road, pulls out of the shady forest, and starts contouring along chaparral-covered slopes. A few black oaks provide intermittent shade. After two miles of walking, you cross the Garnet Peak

Trail. A sharp left takes you up along a wind-blown, manzanita-clothed slope on a trail with many ball-bearing-like rocks.

The view from the boulder pile at Garnet Peak's summit is stupendous—so be sure to carry your camera and a wide-angle lens with you. On three sides the peak falls away sharply to the desert floor. Look for the blue arc of the Salton Sea to the northeast. One word of caution here: on windy days make certain you have a good grip on the rocks!

Yucca on Garnet Peak

THE DESERT EXPERIENCE

If California is the quintessential land of contrasts, then San Diego County is a microcosm of exactly that. The eastern quarter of the county, profiled in this section, represents the hot, dry end of the geographical spectrum. Here, along the eastern edge of the coastal Peninsular Ranges and extending out toward the Salton Sea and beyond, is some of the lowest, hottest and loneliest real estate in America.

The impression that many people have on seeing this desert for the first time is distinctly negative. It appears stark and somehow alien—not consistent with their concept of a green planet Earth. But given the chance, the desert will reveal its mysteries and charms to those who are open-minded enough to explore it.

Try spending a day hiking in the desert. When you strike a path away from your car, and the sound of traffic along the highway fades away,

Silver cholla cactus

you will find yourself deeply involved with the elemental forces of nature around you. Your senses may become sharpened to an extraordinary degree, allowing insights never before experienced. The alien quality of the desert seems reinforced: The sun appears somehow larger than life, pouring radiation upon the shimmering landscape. The air, devoid of moisture, catches in the throat. Brittle, thorny plants cling steadfastly to life, rooted in rock or sand. The diminutive sound of a scurrying animal or alarmed bird cracks the all-pervading silence. All of these impressions contribute to the breadth of the desert experience. But this is not all.

Slowly, but inevitably, comes the realization that the desert isn't really alien and inhospitable. It appears to be lifeless at first glance, yet careful observation reveals evidence of many forms of plant and animal life, active or dormant. The wildflower bloom after spring rains is proof of the regenerative abilities of desert vegetation, and the coming of nightfall brings forth multitudes of nocturnal animals, no matter what the season.

In spite of its sometimes-threatening appearance, the desert can be quite hospitable to human beings. Actually, it is the California desert itself that needs protection from us. Motorcycles and off-road vehicles have legitimate uses on approved routes of travel, but too often the indiscriminate use of these machines by ignorant adventurers upsets the delicate ecological balance and mars the beauty of the desert. Travel by foot, on the other hand, runs a negligible risk of disturbing the fragile environment, and lets you experience most effectively the unique sights, sounds and smells of the desert. By acquiring a sensitivity to the desert environment, you can come to know the desert, and consequently love it.

When traveling in the desert, take plenty of extra water along in the car. Bring a shovel if you intend to turn off the paved roads. Don't underestimate your capacity for drinking water on the trail—it's always safer to bring more than you need. Finally, you may enjoy your desert experience much more by hiking in the early morning or late afternoon, especially on hot days. At times like these, shadows provide welcome relief and the subdued colors of the desert landscape are enhanced by the low sun angle.

Palms at Mountain Palm Springs

Split boulder near Culp Valley

Trip 5
The Anza-Borrego Desert

Facilities and Points of Interest:

Anza-Borrego Visitor Center (767-4205)

Anza-Borrego Desert State Park (767-5311)
developed camp and picnic grounds:

  Borrego Palm Canyon ▲ ⊼
  Tamarisk Grove ▲ ⊼
  Bow Willow ▲ ⊼

Anza-Borrego Desert State Park (767-5311)
primitive camps on or near paved roads:

  Culp Valley ▲
  Arroyo Salado ▲
  Fish Creek ▲
  Yaqui Well ▲
  Blair Valley ▲
  Mountain Palm Springs ▲

San Diego County Parks Department
(565-3600) camp and picnic grounds:

  Vallecito Stage Station ▲ ⊼
  Agua Caliente ▲ ⊼

The Anza-Borrego Desert is truly one of the more extraordinary deserts of the United States. In it you will find nearly every interesting aspect associated with the Colorado Desert of California—that vast expanse of arid land stretching across the foot of California from the Colorado River to the slopes of the Peninsular Ranges.

Most of the western portion of the Colorado Desert, from the mountains to the Salton Sea basin, has the distinction of being included in a state park, the boundaries of which are flung far and wide. The Anza-Borrego Desert State Park is the largest state park in the United States, encompassing nearly a thousand square miles within extreme limits 60 miles long and 30 miles wide. The "low" desert of the Salton Sea sink, with its characteristic badlands, is found here, as well as rugged palm canyons and the serene pinyon-pine and juniper mountains of the "high" desert.

A good network of paved roads, and a much more extensive system of dirt roads suitable for 4-wheel drive vehicles penetrates the interior of the park, allowing quick access (on foot, from the roads) to almost any remote section of the park you wish to explore. I've included 12 trails in this section, an adequate number for the purposes of this book, but a far from complete list of places to see. The backpacker will find almost unlimited prospects. Indeed, as the park literature has stated, it is probable that all the major points of interest in the park have not yet been discovered.

An introduction to the Anza-Borrego Desert would not be complete without a few brief comments on its history. The area has known a succession of human inhabitants in the last few thousand years, as evidenced by shelters and artifacts left behind. Since the drying up of the ancient fresh-water Lake Cahuilla, which occupied the present-day Salton Sea, Kumeyaay and Cahuilla Indians had populated oases and canyons fed by water that was more plentiful than today. The Indians were nomadic, traveling in small bands, and occupying various camping sites according to the season. Fruit, foliage and fiber from low desert plants and the pinyon pine and oak of higher elevations provided the raw materials for survival in a harsh environment. Small-game hunting and trading with other tribes rounded out their lifestyle. Archaeologically significant Indian sites are common in the Anza-Borrego today, and it is likely that many have not yet been discovered.

The late eighteenth century saw the first attempts to establish a land route connecting the Spanish settlements and missions at Sonora, Mexico, to the coast of California. Juan Bautista de Anza was the first Spaniard to do so. His passage included a trek across Borrego Valley and Coyote Canyon, two well-known areas of the park. Earlier, Pedro Fages had descended into the Anza-Borrego area from the mountains to the west, thus claiming credit for the first journey by Europeans into the California desert. Incidentally, the *Borrego* part of the name Anza-Borrego comes from the Spanish word for bighorn sheep. Anza's historic trail across the desert has been erased over time, but sightings of bighorn sheep are still quite common, especially in the park's remote mountains and steep canyons.

In the middle of the nineteenth century, the so-called Southern Emigrant Trail through Carrizo Corridor (the series of valleys roughly paralleling County Highway S-2 in the southern half of the park) and San Felipe Valley bore the traffic of gold-seeking California pioneers.

The turn of the twentieth century saw some grazing and agriculture in the broad valleys and basins of the present park area. Finally, in 1928, state authorities, seeking to preserve a representative expanse of southern desert, chose this area because of its outstanding natural features. An aggressive acquisition program has continued to the present day, the result being a 620,000-acre Anza-Borrego Desert State Park.

If your's is a first visit, you'd best head for the town of Borrego Springs and the nearby Anza-Borrego Desert State Park visitor center. Curiously, the town of Borrego Springs and most of Borrego Valley surrounding it, is not included in the park. It's a political "island" of privately owned land—a large hole within the park. The small business district around Christmas Circle in the middle of town has lodging and all the usual businesses associated with a small resort town.

Two main entrances serve Borrego Springs and the northern half of the park. You can take Highway 78 east from Julian, descend the Banner Grade to San Felipe Valley and enter the park by way of Tamarisk Grove Campground. You then turn north on County Highway S-3, go over Yaqui Pass, and make a long glide into Borrego Valley below. Alternately, you can drive north from Santa Ysabel on Highway 79 past Lake Henshaw to County Highway S-2, continue east as County Highway S-22 goes left, and finally negotiate the spectacular Montezuma Grade into Borrego Valley.

Trip 5: Anza-Borrego Desert

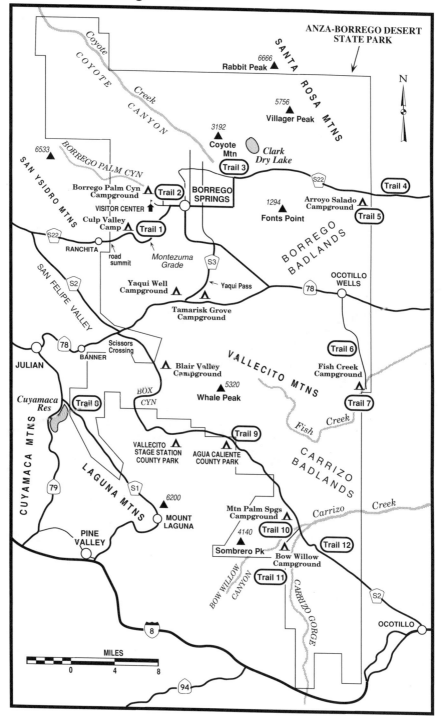

The north half of the park is more popular, and includes major attractions like the below-ground Visitor Center and the impressive Borrego Palm Canyon. Coyote Canyon and its tributaries in the northwest corner of the park are a favorite of adventurous souls, but access is challenging, even for those using 4-wheel drive vehicles.

The convoluted Borrego Badlands, east of Borrego Springs, are an example of the most barren and forbidding kind of desert in California. A four-mile-long sandy road going south from Borrego-Salton Seaway (S-22) can take you to the spectacular overlook of Fonts Point—but access is problematical for many standard passenger cars.

The southern half of the park is relatively neglected, but for no good reason. County Highway S-2, running southeast from Highway 78 to Interstate 8 at Ocotillo, allows ready access to the boulder-heaped mountains and sand-drowned valleys along the southwest side of the park. The major state park campground of the south half, Bow Willow Campground, is located along this road, as are two county parks, Old Vallecito Stage Station and Agua Caliente Springs.

The sun-blasted Carrizo Badlands, east of Highway S-2, not only contain outstanding eroded landscapes, but also fossil beds comprising, as one paleontologist puts it, "one of the most remarkably complete sequences of animal life to be found anywhere in the world."

The wide-open spaces of Anza-Borrego are the last frontier of San Diego County. Nowhere else will you find the same kind of peace, silence, and splendid emptiness. We must be thankful to those who had (and still have) the foresight to protect them from exploitation.

Borrego Badlands from Fonts Point

Trip 5, Trail 1
Culp Valley Vista Point

Approximate Distance: 1 mile
 out and back
Low point (trailhead): 3340 feet
High point (Vista Point): 3520 feet

Of all the roads leading into the Anza-Borrego Desert State Park, the Montezuma Highway, or Montezuma Grade (County S-22), makes the most spectacular approach. From Ranchita, the road literally carves through rock in the ten-mile descent to Borrego Valley. Several turnouts are provided along the road for those who like to gape at the scenery. If you want to enjoy a view of the desert floor without the noise and distraction of passing traffic, there's a better view point accessible by way of a short trail starting at Culp Valley primitive campground.

The campground is located north of the highway approximately three miles east of the summit on S-22 that marks the park boundary. Park at the far end of the campground and walk north on an eroded dirt road—now a trail—leading up to the ridge dividing Culp Valley from the Hellhole Canyon drainage. Atop the ridge, you briefly join a branch of the California Riding and Hiking Trail. The vista point lies about 400 yards to the east, on top of a high spot on the ridge.

The San Ysidro Mountains, capped by a series of cone-like peaks (the largest of which is known as The Thimble), rears up to the north and west, while Borrego Valley shimmers

below at the mouth of appropriately named Hellhole Canyon. You are standing nearly 3000 feet above the valley floor at this point, and the photographic possibilities are manifold.

For a bit of added adventure, you might try returning by way of Pena Spring, which is well hidden in shrubbery on a slope overlooking the South Fork of Hellhole Canyon. A pipe here dispenses cool, delicious water. The spring has long been considered one of the better sources of water in Anza-Borrego, both for travelers and the native wildlife.

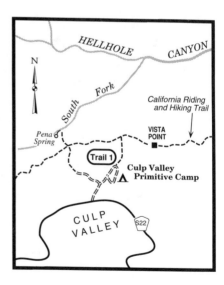

View from Culp Valley Vista

70

Trip 5, Trail 2
Borrego Palm Canyon

Approximate distance: 3 miles
 out and back
Low point (trailhead): 840 feet
High point (palm oasis): 1250 feet

Hiking the Borrego Palm Canyon Nature Trail is simply the best prerequisite for further exploration in Anza-Borrego. Aside from gaping at the canyon walls which rise impressively on both sides, you'll learn to recognize many of the common types of vegetation characteristic of Anza-Borrego's mountain-desert interface. The highlight is, of course, the large grove of native *Washingtonia filifera* fan palm trees at the end of the trail— a popular place for photographers. This palm oasis is by far, Anza-Borrego's most popular hiking destination, sought after by thousands on some springtime days; yet even here you can find solitude if you come out in the heat of a summer afternoon and hike the trail while the

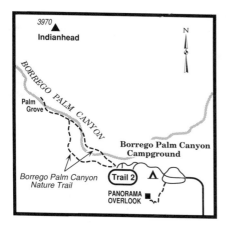

sun sinks behind the mountains to the west.

Palm canyons are not unique to the Anza-Borrego Desert. Native palms are scattered throughout the Colorado Desert—especially in the well-watered canyons on the east-facing slopes of the highest mountain ranges. By number alone, Borrego Palm Canyon cannot boast of the thousands of palms that line the canyons south of Palm Springs or the bigger canyons of Baja's Sierra Juarez and Sierra San Pedro Martir. But you won't easily find a better display that's both easily accessible and remote from the sights and sounds of civilization.

You'll find the trailhead in the west corner of the sprawling Borrego Palm Canyon Campground, north of the new Anza-Borrego Visitor Center, and northwest of Borrego Springs. A small fee covers picnicking or hiking for the day. Be sure to pick up the informative leaflet for the trail, as it describes many of the common types of cacti, shrubs and trees indigenous to this and other canyons of the Colorado Desert. Descriptions of wildlife and geological formations are included also.

In the first mile, the trail winds gradually upward across an alluvial fan at the mouth of the canyon. You'll catch a glimpse of the palms just before entering the V-shaped gorge. The first sight of these tightly clustered palms on a bright, sunny day is quite startling. Contrasting with the warm colors of the canyon walls, the stark green palm fronds crowning each trunk seem to give off their own radiant light.

Like all palm oases, this one is supported by a year-round supply of water—on the surface or underground—seeping across the palms' shallow roots. By midsummer the water often dries up on the surface, but the underground seepage continues.

The maintained nature trail comes to an end at the first and largest of the several palm groves that line the canyon. Beyond that, boulder-hopping is the means for further travel. On the return, you have your choice of taking an alternate trail, branching off the main trail near the mouth of the canyon. This slightly longer return route winds amid the tall, thorny ocotillos that thrive on a higher part of the alluvial fan. Drab most of the year, these ocotillos light up with flag-like, red blossom-clusters at the branch tips a few weeks after their roots receive a good soaking.

Borrego Palm Canyon

Trip 5, Trail 3
Coyote Mountain

**Approximate distance: 6 miles
  out and back**
Low point (trailhead): 620 feet
High point: 1620 feet

Coyote Mountain stands at the northeast corner of Borrego Valley. As seen from the valley, it presents a surface no less brown and wrinkled than elephant hide. In spite of its lack of inherent attractiveness, it does offer some excellent vantage points for viewing and photographing the vast sweep of the desert floor and the mountains that rise so abruptly from it.

An old jeep road going up along the south spur of Coyote Mountain offers an easy approach for hikers. You start at Pegleg Smith Monument, at the base of Coyote Mountain, where Highway S-22 from Borrego Springs makes a wide turn to the east. At the monument, you'll find a large pile of rocks—a monument to a legendary desert wanderer and the legend of his lost gold. Adding ten

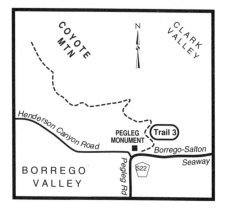

stones, so the story goes, will bring you good luck in finding gold nuggets; removing any will have exactly the opposite effect.

Start by walking eastward along the base of the mountain, where you should find the old roadbed. Once you gain the ridge, you'll feel like you're halfway into the sky. Clark Valley and its normally dry lakebed to the east stand at the base of the starkly eroded Santa Rosa Mountains, and the Borrego Salton Seaway skims across the sand toward the Salton Sea and Imperial Valley.

Soon, the entire Borrego Valley comes into view, seemingly at your feet. Nestled against the San Ysidro Mountains in the west you see the defocused town of Borrego Springs, which sprawls across many square miles. The De Anza Desert Country Club makes a green splotch against the mountain front, and fields lined with tamarisk windbreaks form a checkerboard pattern in the foreground.

Some three miles from the monument, the old jeep road fades. You've now climbed a thousand feet above the valley floor—a good place to turn back if you're either tired or unprepared for anything further. Peripatetic hikers might want to continue another 2 miles up along Coyote

Mountain's ridge to the 3,192-foot summit.

This walk is best during the "cool" days of winter, when the thermometer rises no farther than the 60s and 70s in the daytime. There is no shade whatsoever on the mountain. Carry binoculars for the long view, but don't neglect to scan the ground at your feet. Pegleg's lost gold is out there somewhere!

San Ysidro Mountains from Coyote Mountain

74

Trip 5, Trail 4
Calcite Mine

Approximate distance: 4 miles
 round trip
Low point (trailhead): 600 feet
High Point (Calcite Mine): 1140 feet

The Calcite Mine area is a twisted, tortured landscape caused by sedimentary rock being raised, tilted and crushed against the rising Santa Rosa Mountains. Untold millennia of cutting and polishing by water and wind erosion have produced the chaotic rock formations and slotlike canyons you'll have the pleasure of exploring in the immediate area.

During World War II, optical-grade calcite crystals were mined here for use in bomb sights. Trench-mining operations have left deep scars upon the earth, seemingly as fresh today as when they were made. This is a very graphic illustration of the slow process by which nature can heal its wounds—in this unusual case, only by further erosion.

An old jeep road—the Calcite Road—negotiable by some vehicles, leads directly to the mine site, but I'm assuming you'll be walking, not driving it. There's a small parking area where the old road meets Borrego-Salton Seaway, one mile west of the large microwave tower marking the park's east boundary and the Imperial County line.

Follow the Calcite Road down into the South Fork of Palm Wash, and back up the other side. For a while, the road runs right along the lip of a bluff overlooking Palm Wash and one of its tributaries. Carefully peer over at the drainage pattern below you, for on the return you'll be traveling these same labyrinthine gorges. Dipping momentarily, Calcite Road

Calcite Mine area

crosses the above-mentioned tributary ravine and continues another half mile to the mine site. There, calcite crystals glitter in the sunlight. Veins of calcite can still be found along the walls of some of the manmade trenches.

The return trip, including the diversion through Palm Wash, allows a very different perspective. Palm Wash lies a short distance east from the mine, but you can't climb down to it because of its steepness and depth. Instead, return to the aforementioned tributary ravine about one-half mile back down the road, and then proceed down-canyon along the ravine bottom. As you descend, the ravine cuts ever deeper into the underlying sandstone until it becomes a deep gorge—almost a "fat-man's misery" situation. When you reach the jumbled boulders and sandstone blocks in Palm Wash at the mouth of the tributary, walk downstream one-quarter mile to a jeep trail going up the right-hand slope. It takes you back to Calcite Road.

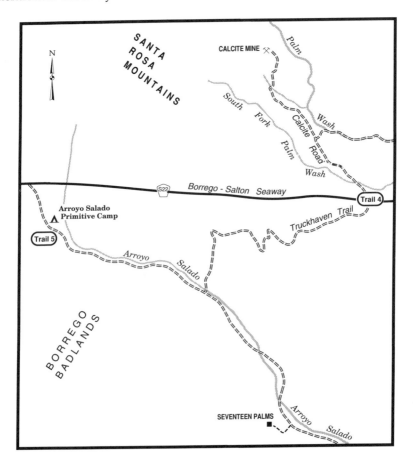

Seventeen Palms oasis

Trip 5, Trail 5
Seventeen Palms Oasis

Approximate distance: 6 miles
out and back
Low point (Seventeen Palms): 410 feet
High point (trailhead): 900 feet

The small oasis at Seventeen Palms on the edge of the Borrego Badlands has some long-celebrated legends associated with it. Most tell of desperately dehydrated prospectors falling swollen-tongued on the meager seeps of saline water beneath the palms, and narrowly avoiding death by drinking whatever they could. Aside from its contribution to the desert mystique, Seventeen Palms has for thousands of years played a crucial role in the survival of many kinds of wildlife in this part of the desert.

The hike to Seventeen Palms along Arroyo Salado can be pleasant on a cool day. Carry a canteen, since the water at the oasis is not potable, except, of course, in cases of extreme emergency. Most of the hike is along an auto road recommended for 4-wheel drive only, so you can shorten the distance greatly if you have that kind of vehicle.

If you park in the area of Arroyo Salado primitive camp, you can drive in about a half-mile from the Borrego-Salton Seaway to where the road usually deteriorates. From there, simply follow Arroyo Salado wash about three miles southeast to a parking area and foot trail leading to the palms.

At Seventeen Palms you'll discover the "prospectors' post office." Decades ago, prospectors and travelers used the oasis as a point to relay messages. Today this tradition continues, and you will probably find hundreds of notes and business cards in a barrel beneath the palms.

Orcutt aster

Trip 5, Trail 6
Elephant Trees Area

Approximate distance: 1.2 miles
  for the loop
Elevation: approximately 230 feet

The harsh environment of the desert has helped initiate the evolution of many unusual species of plants and animals that are now perfectly adapted to arid conditions. A good example is the elephant tree (*Bursera microphylla*), which makes a sparse and scattered appearance in the Anza-Borrego Desert. Though common south of the border, so rare are specimens of this plant north of the border that rumors from the early 1900s of their existence in the park area were not confirmed until 1937. Today they're a recognized park attraction.

To reach the Elephant Trees Area, drive 6 miles south on Split Mountain Road from Highway 78 at Ocotillo Wells. A dirt road, negotiable with care by standard cars, goes a mile west to the trailhead and parking area for the Elephant Trees Discovery Trail. The trail passes through a dry wash and loops around a boulder-strewn slope where many modest-sized elephant trees reside.

You'll recognize these trees immediately as botanical oddities. They're characterized by short stubby trunks, puffy limbs, reddish twigs and sap, green foliage and blue fruit. Some measure about 10 feet in height and 15 feet in breadth. Like desert succulents, elephant trees are able to store water internally and thus survive during months-long periods of utter drought.

Elephant tree

79

Trip 5, Trail 7
Split Mountain-Fish Creek

Approximate one-way distances
from Fish Creek primitive camp:
  3.5 miles to Mud Hills Wash
  4.5 miles to Oyster Shell Wash
Approximate Elevations:
  Split Mountain, 400 feet
  Mud Hills Wash, 550 feet
  Head of Oyster Shell Wash, 1200 feet

Like some ancient Biblical catastrophe, Split Mountain appears to have been pulled apart by some almighty force on high. In reality, though, the forces have come from within the earth and have occurred in a more or less orderly fashion for the past few million years. The beginning of that period saw the present Fish Creek and Split Mountain area submerged in what was then an extension of the Gulf of California. Many layers of sediment were deposited there, and later uplifted when the land west of the present Salton Sea rose. Erosion, mostly by water flowing during flash floods through a gap in the sediments, has performed most of the excavation we see in Split Mountain today. Tectonic movements, and the occasional earthquakes they spawn, have helped to loosen things up now and again. You will be convinced of this when you see how fractured and unstable the walls of Split Mountain are.

Choosing your starting point for exploration of Split Mountain and the closer tributaries of Fish Creek may well depend upon the condition of the primitive roads that go through them and the type of vehicle

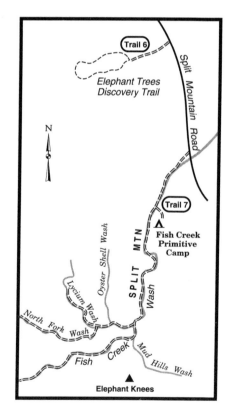

Split Mountain entrance

you drive. We'll assume you can get your vehicle into Fish Creek primitive camp at the entrance to Split Mountain. Four-wheel drive and high-clearance vehicles regularly make the journey through on the silt and sand of Fish Creek wash, but I suggest that walking through is far more aesthetically rewarding. I've walked through the gorge on a full-moon night, when nothing stirs except hooting owls, and spooky shadows cast by the angular walls stab across Fish Creek's broad, flat floor.

The first thing you'll notice on entering the gorge is the series of vertical cracks and shifted strata along the west wall. Here and there, fresh debris lies at the bottom of some of the steep ravines or near overhanging cliffs. Some of the larger piles were the result of a 1968 earthquake—reason enough to heed rangers' advice not to camp directly beneath any steep cliffs. Farther on, to the right, you may notice an anticline of sandstone layers bent over in an inverted U—this the result of unimaginable pressures and stresses applied to them deep within the earth.

Beyond Split Mountain, Fish Creek wash splits into several forks and tributaries. When you reach the first fork, you may either continue south on Fish Creek wash to Mud Hills Wash, or take the North Fork wash west to Oyster Shell Wash.

The mud hills, as the term suggests, are the barren and smoothly eroded remnants of mud sediments deposited on a former sea floor. A half-mile walk down Mud Hills Wash gives you a good view of these hills, which sparkle with gypsum crystals. From here there's also a good view of the feature called Elephant Knees on the nearby, dark-colored butte. On the south and west sides of this butte, you can find fossil-shell reefs loaded with the remains of marine organisms.

If you head for Oyster Shell Wash, a tributary of Fish Creek's North Fork, continue up the drainage as far as you can go. There you'll find water-polished sandstone walls and shallow depressions sometimes filled with water. Keep your eyes open for oyster-shell fossils, too.

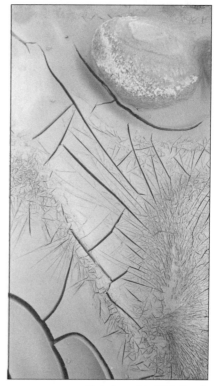

Dried mud in Fish Creek

Mud Hills Wash

Oyster Shell Wash

Trip 5, Trail 8
Pedro Fages Trail

Approximate distance: 9 miles one way
Low point (Mason Valley): 2310 feet
High point (near Cuyamaca Reservoir):
  4790 feet

In 1772, Pedro Fages started east from San Diego in pursuit of deserters from the presidio. His initial travels took him straight into the unknown interior mountains and deserts of present-day San Diego County, and resulted in the discovery of two important land routes through the Anza-Borrego Desert. Fages and his men made their way down to the desert on an Indian trail through Oriflamme Canyon, the first official entry into the Colorado Desert by the Spaniards. He then left the desert by a northern passage through Coyote Canyon, which was rediscovered two years later by Anza and his party of settlers.

Fossil shell

Today, a branch of the California Riding and Hiking Trail from Cuyamaca Reservoir in the Cuyamaca Mountains to Mason Valley and Box Canyon in the Anza-Borrego Desert roughly follows Fages' historical descent through Oriflamme Canyon. This nine-mile segment, which ties together existing dirt roads and foot paths, is suitable for a one-way trek if transportation is arranged at both ends. In the downhill direction, west to east, the 2400-foot descent should take no more than about 4 hours. In the meantime, your transportation crew can make the journey by car through Julian and Banner to the pre-arranged rendezvous point in the desert. While browsing in Julian, of course, they shouldn't forget to pick up some cold apple cider for your arrival at the end of the trail!

Topside in the Cuyamacas, you can park alongside the Pedro Fages monument on Highway S-l, east of Highway 79. Walk about 300 yards west on the highway to the cattle grate where you pick up the California Riding and Hiking Trail going east through a gate. It skirts a meadow and eventually comes up to road—Mason Valley Truck Trail, where you turn right. The Riding and Hiking Trail splits here, the left branch going northward down Chariot Canyon, and the right branch going east toward Highway S-2. A seldom-maintained section of the Pacific Crest Trail also passes through the area on its way from the Laguna Mountains toward Scissors Crossing at Highways S-2 and 78.

A moderately steep descent, then a level stretch on the road precede a sharp drop down Oriflamme Canyon's north wall. At the bottom, the trail emerges upon the more gentle terrain of Mason Valley, and various cacti and desert shrubs appear in ever-increasing numbers.

A good place to end the hike is the Box Canyon historical site along Highway S-2. To get there, you leave Mason Valley Truck Trail at a point along the base of Granite Mountain, and follow a segment of the Riding and Hiking Trail to the other side of S-2 on up to the Box Canyon monument.

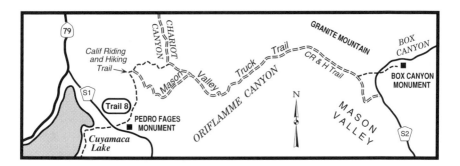

Trip 5, Trail 9
Moonlight Canyon Trail

Approximate distance: 1.5 miles for the loop
Low point (trailhead): 1310 feet
High point: 1650 feet

To me, sunrise on the desert gives a sense of absolute quiet and stillness. The sun cautiously peeps over the eastern horizon and silent shadows recede in an age-old ritual of rebirth. For a brief hour or two, cool air from the previous night clings to the ground, and the true colors of rocks and minerals are not diminished by the harsh glare of the midday sun.

The trail through Moonlight Canyon is one that is best suited for early morning exploration. You will find it at Agua Caliente County Park, a popular camping area off County Highway S-2. Be sure to bring a bathing suit, so that you can enjoy a dip in the warm waters of Agua Caliente's outdoor or indoor hot-spring pools before or after your hike.

The trail starts at the south perimeter of the campground, climbs up and over a saddle, runs down Moonlight Canyon, and circles back down to the campground. During the stillness of the early morning, you can get a sense of moisture in the canyon bottom before you come upon some small seeps there. At the trail's high point, you'll be treated to a fine view of the Vallecito Mountains to the north. Morning or late afternoon sunlight shines low and obliquely across the face of these mountains, creating a classic desert panorama.

Vallecito Mountains

87

Trip 5, Trail 10
Mountain Palm Springs

Approximate distance: 1 mile (one way)
to Palm Bowl Grove; 1.5 miles (one way)
to Torote Bowl
Low point (trailhead): 760 feet
High point (Torote Bowl): 1320 feet

The scattered groves of palms at Mountain Palm Springs are yet another example of palm oases thriving in the midst of an otherwise desiccated mountain range. Though not as spectacular as Borrego Palm Canyon to the north, this area has nevertheless suffered far less from trampling by human footsteps, and it remains in a more natural state.

You start hiking at Mountain Palm Springs primitive camp, one-half mile off County S-2 at a point about two miles north of Bow Willow Campground. You have the choice of following either or both of two shallow washes. In the north wash, you pass directly by the little group of palms at Surprise Canyon Grove

and a bit farther come upon the magnificent Palm Bowl Grove, its dozens of palms tightly clustered together.

The south wash takes you past Pygmy Grove to Southwest Grove and its conspicuous waterhole. A catch-basin lined with rocks has been built here to provide a good water source for the local wildlife which, aside from birds, usually consists of coyotes, jackrabbits, and bighorn sheep. For a look at some elephant trees in the vicinity, follow the signs from Southwest Grove to Torote Bowl. Here, on a rocky hillside, you'll find that botanical oddity known as *torote* in Baja—and "elephant tree" north of the border.

From Southwest Grove, it is possible to head south on a trail to Bow Willow Campground, or north across a rocky slope over to Surprise Canyon Grove. Another trail leads north over a saddle near Palm Bowl Grove into Indian Gorge, a popular area for car camping.

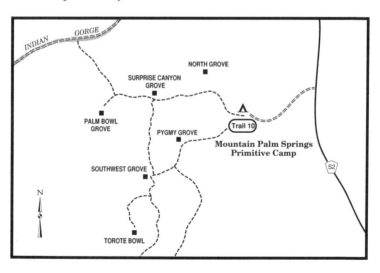

Southwest Grove

Trip 5, Trail 11
Bow Willow Canyon-
Rockhouse Canyon

Approximate distance: 7 miles round trip
Low point (trailhead): 1020 feet
High point: 1740 feet

Fill up your canteens for this one. You'll tread many a mile of jagged, rocky terrain utterly devoid of water. Also advisable are sturdy boots and long pants to protect you against the desert agave and cholla cactus which grow in abundance here.

Begin at Bow Willow Campground, about two miles west of Highway S-2 down a good road of hard-packed sand. Park and stroll past the campsites onto the sands that cover the bottom of Bow Willow Canyon. Continue nearly one-half mile to where a small ravine comes down from the south canyon wall. You begin the loop portion of this trip here, by scrambling up this ravine.

About one-half mile up is a single palm tree, its dead fronds matted snugly against its trunk. Here, then, is a palm canyon with only one palm tree. Afterward, the obstacle course of granite boulders gets tougher. Then, suddenly, the going is easy as a wide, sandy wash leads you gently upward to a plateau of broken rock formations and cactus gardens. It's easy to lose the trail at this point, so watch carefully for trail markers— usually little piles of rocks called ducks or cairns.

After about two miles of meandering through the rocky landscape, the trail goes down onto the Rockhouse Canyon wash and continues up-canyon to an old rock shelter once used by cattlemen. You'll find it nestled against a boulder on the south side of the canyon. If the midday sun beats down unmercifully, it's a cool spot for a rest or a picnic. If there's been plentiful rain, you'll find some lively little cascades of water in a ravine behind the rock house.

From the rock house, another trail leads north over a low spot in the

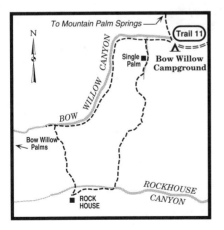

divide between Rockhouse and Bow Willow canyons. Once over the summit, you drop quickly to the floor of Bow Willow Canyon. At this point you can head straight back to the campground by way of the gently sloping, sandy floor of Bow Willow Canyon—or you can elect to do some further exploring in upper Bow Willow Canyon. Palms line two forks of the canyon about one and a half miles west.

Old rock house

Trip 5, Trail 12
Canyon Sin Nombre

Approximate distance: 5 miles out and back
Low point (Canyon Sin Nombre): 760 feet
High point (trailhead): 1210 feet

Nowhere else in the desert will you find the raw erosive power of flash flooding better illustrated than in the badlands. Stripped of vegetation and acted upon by the opposing forces of geologic uplift and gravity-induced drainage, the sandstone and mud cliffs of the badlands offer mute testimony of their creation. This is exactly what you'll witness in Canyon Sin Nombre—"Canyon without a Name."

The primitive road into the canyon begins on Highway S-2, three miles south of the spur road into Bow Willow Campground. The road starts in soft sand (definitely a trap for most passenger cars) and heads immediately downhill toward a flat area at the entrance to the canyon. Barrel cacti dot the flats and the nearby rocky slopes, some growing to heights of five feet. Notice how most lean slightly to the south, toward the sun at midday.

A mile from the starting point, you enter the canyon. Inside, jagged, metamorphic rock rises sharply. This hard rock is soon replaced by softer sedimentary rock in the canyon walls—sandstone and mudstone, some of it contorted into swirling patterns.

When the canyon starts widening, keep a close eye on the smooth, convoluted walls on the left side. Don't

Slot canyon off Canyon Sin Nombre

93

miss the vertical-walled tributary ravine on the left. Enter its portals, and (for the sure-footed only) start climbing up the gorge as it narrows to a veritable crevasse-like slot.

You may feel like you're groping toward an uncertain destination, but soon the passage widens and you eventually emerge atop the bluff overlooking Canyon Sin Nombre. All around is what seems to be total desolation. In the clear desert air, your depth perception is warped, so that anything beyond close range seems like it's pasted onto the horizon, like the background of an old movie set.

Let your imagination take wing, but don't lose track of your footsteps! There's only one easy way to return to Canyon Sin Nombre—the way you came.

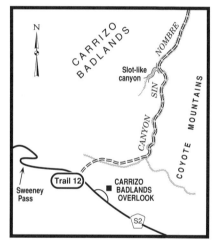

Young barrel cactus

Above Canyon Sin Nombre

A Note to the Reader

In the pages of this book, by means of words and pictures, I have attempted to give you a taste of what you can discover in certain parts of San Diego's big and diverse back yard.

The earliest edition of *Backcountry Roads and Trails, San Diego County* was the first guidebook written on the subject of San Diego County hiking trails. Material for the first edition was researched in 1974-75, and the book appeared in 1977. This current (fourth edition) version has been completely updated, although nothing fundamentally new has been added to its content during the intervening years. It remains, I hope, a book of low cost containing useful information about some of the better hikes in our local mountain and desert areas.

Backcountry Roads and Trails predated by several years the debut of my more comprehensive *Afoot and Afield in San Diego County*, which was published by Wilderness Press of Berkeley, California in 1986. In 1992 *Afoot and Afield in San Diego County* was extensively revised and expanded, and it now contains detailed descriptions and maps of 192 hiking trips covering all of San Diego's public recreation lands from the coast to the desert.

If you have enjoyed following—or have been intrigued by—the trips described in this book, I'm sure you will be even more satisfied by the information contained in the latest *Afoot and Afield in San Diego County*. The book is widely available in bookstores and other outlets throughout San Diego.

—Jerry Schad

About the Author

Jerry Schad, a fifth-generation Californian, has lived in San Diego County since 1972. He has been a columnist for various San Diego-area publications since 1982, and he currently writes a weekly outdoor column for the San Diego *Reader*. Jerry also holds a position in the Physical Science Department at San Diego Mesa College, and teaches introductory physical science and astronomy courses there.